GAIA'S DANCE
THE STORY OF EARTH & US

A CHILDREN'S BOOK FOR GROWNUPS

Elisabet Sahtouris

For everyone helping to rebalance Gaia's dance toward a world of trust and love

ISBN: 1983530093

ISBN-13: 978-1983530098

Contents

Preface
From Ancient Myth
To
Modern Science

Everything I say in this book is my personal view of Earth's evolution and human history within its context. As an evolution biologist, I think of myself as a deep 'pastist' in order to be a good futurist. When we come to understand our roots in the evolutionary past, it becomes easier to see the possibilities for our future.

Increasing complexity is the way of Nature over time, so it is not easy to tell the scientific story of nearly four billion years of evolution and the past few thousand years of human history in a relatively short book. It takes a great deal of simplification and conversion into coherent story. That is why I have chosen to tell this story as a children's book for grownups—to make the complex as simple as possible.

Even what we think of as 'facts' can change over time. Science makes new discoveries, new theories, new explanations and even changes those beliefs on which it is built. Yes, science itself—its theories, hypotheses, experiments, results and interpretations of those results—rests on a foundational story of the nature of our universe and how we can study it to get reliable information about it. No one can make a theory without any idea of what that theory is meant to explain.

So scientists must believe in their ideas of what a universe is before they can begin their work of studying it. And, to complicate things in yet another way, scientists are changing their minds about what kind of universe they believe in, as you will see in this book. I am among the scientists changing their views from a non-living meaningless universe to a conscious intelligent universe, as you will also see.

I have chosen to tell this Story of Earth & Us as though our Earth is a real-if-mythological being: Gaia. She is the ancient Greek goddess whose name is still the name Earth in the Greek language. In our own times her name has also—thanks to English scientist James Lovelock and his author neighbor William Golding—come to stand for the scientifically discovered living nature of Earth. Gaia's story is what makes this a children's book for grownups. I hope it will give you a new sense of yourself as a vital part of her dance!

Elisabet Sahtouris, Mallorca 2015

Introduction: From Ancient Myth to Modern Science

From the very earliest times, people have told stories about how Earth and all its living creatures came to be. One of the oldest and loveliest of these stories is the ancient Greek myth of Gaia's Dance.

In ancient times, Greek families gathered together outdoors on warm summer evenings and listened to wandering storytellers who walked from village to village. "Once upon a time," the storyteller would say, "so long ago it was even before the very beginning of things, there was only a great, dark emptiness." His hand swept the sky, as though to wipe out all the colors of the sunset. "No skies," he went on, "no seas or mountains, no people or animals. No world at all. Just the vast, yawning emptiness called Chaos. And that's how it was for a very long time."

"Then," he continued, "Something happened. Something stirred in this Chaos; something began to move… If you had been there to see, it might have looked at first like a dim, swirling mist. But as it came out of the darkness, you would have seen the mist turn slowly into white veils wrapped around a beautiful dancing goddess: the Goddess Gaia!

"The lovely Gaia danced round and round in spirals, there in the midst of darkness, without anything to dance upon, without anywhere to touch down her feet." "As Gaia danced faster and faster," he went on, "her whirling body formed itself into mountains and valleys. Sweat poured from her body and began to pool as seas. Round and round she whirled, dancer and dance in one. Her graceful arms stirred up a wind that blew and grew into a cloud-rich sky. She named this wind-sky 'Ouranos' and wrapped him around herself as a loving mate.

"Dancing on and on, with Ouranos to protect her, Gaia became Earth, with its forests and rivers, fishes and birds and animals, and the giant Titans who were Gaia's first two-legged children. From these giants, in the course of time, all the gods and goddesses and all the people of Earth were born.

"Gaia knew that people are creatures curious to know how things began and how they will continue" he went on, "so she let her secrets flow from special places, such as Delphi, where an oracle reads and interprets them."

"Remember always that Gaia's Dance, however people remember it, was the beginning of the world—of all nature, of all people. We still feel her presence—in the seas, in the sky, in every mountain, every creature and in our hearts. She is the great Mother of All, giver and protector of life. If we love her as our mother, respect and care for her, then the dance of our own lives will become as beautiful and harmonious as hers."

In our own time today, we are still curious to know how Earth came to be and what will happen to our beautiful planet and to us and our own children and their children off into the future. But when people want to know about things like the creation of Earth and its creatures today, they usually listen to scientists instead of wandering storytellers. Still, sometimes even scientists are surprised to discover things that remind them of ancient tales such as the myth of Gaia's Dance.

Until quite recently, scientists were sure the only thing alive about Earth was its 'biological life'—the plants and all the creatures from microbes to mammoths. Mountains, seas, skies—everything that seemed to be part of the planet itself—were thought to have been formed from non-living matter in ways that had nothing to do with life. Life was supposed to have come into being on a ready-made non-living Earth.

This, of course, left scientists with a very great mystery to solve: How could life begin on a non-living planet?

The more we study Earth, the stranger and more wonderful are the things we learn about it. Our newest discovery is that Earth itself behaves like a wondrous great being that is as alive as our own bodies!

Most native peoples of the world saw and respected Earth as their mother, but for modern scientists, the discovery that Earth is alive is still quite new. When one of them—James Lovelock—named this living Earth "Gaia" in memory of the ancient Greek myth, other scientists found that strange. But every day scientists are learning more about Gaia in her creative dance, in the ways her creatures form and dance together. With this new knowledge, scientists are piecing together a realistic, modern story of Gaia's Dance—and that is what this book is about.

Gaia's dance of creation is what we have come to know as Earth's evolution, and we now call the harmonious balance of this dance ecology. Like our own bodies, Gaia keeps herself at just the right temperature for life. And just as our bodies work to keep the right balance among all the atoms and molecules, the chemicals in our skin and blood and bones and organs, so does Earth work to keep the right chemical balance in its skies and seas, its rocks and soils.

We will see that the ancient myth foretold the scientific story in just the right order: first the formation of Earth's body, then the pooling of the seas, followed by the creation of the atmosphere and finally the appearance of plants and animals, including ourselves. The scientific story is even more fascinating, in all its details, than the ancient myth.

Some details of this story, which you are about to read, will change even by the time you read them because new things will continue to be discovered about Gaia every day and in all the years to come. Perhaps you will help find new pieces of the story, or bring those we know up to date. We are all a part of Gaia's Dance, so the more we learn about it, the more we learn about ourselves as people of Earth.

The first thing we learn is that we people are still very new Gaian creatures who still have much to learn about balancing ourselves within the dance of our beautiful planet.

Human history seems very long to us when we study all that has happened in it. But humans have been a part of Gaia's dance for only a very few million years, while Gaia has been dancing for thousands of millions of years.   That means we are among her youngest creatures, and perhaps helps explain why we humans are acting rather like children making foolish mistakes as we try to grow up.

Actually, we are not the first of Gaia's children to make problems for themselves and for Gaia, as we will see, but there is something special about us—we are, as far as we know, the first of her children who can understand such problems, think about them, turn them into stories and solve them by our own free choice.

The biggest problem we have created, in addition to war and hunger for many of our own kind, is damage to Gaia's body, what we call her ecosystems, the regional parts of her land, oceans and atmosphere with all their creatures. Yet each of us depends on the health of these ecosystems as much as each of the cells in our bodies depends on the rest of our body for its life.

The problems we have created are now so big that we know them as 'global crises' and many people think we will never be able to solve them. Yet just at this time in our troubled world, our eyes are opening to see Gaia and to recognize her thousands of millions of years of experience in solving both big and small problems. We can look to her for advice and help, as though she really were the Great Mother of whom the ancient storyteller told. If we do, we can learn from her experience and wisdom, so that we humans may grow up wise enough to make a happier world.

In the ancient myth, as we heard, people discovered Gaia's secrets in special places such as Delphi, where they went to learn them and to see what the future held. Now, just when we really need to learn them, they seem to be flowing from Gaia's body almost everywhere scientists are looking. So, let's go on now to see just how we discovered Gaia, what her dance has been like until now, and how we might dance less destructively and more harmoniously and creatively with her into our own future.

- 1 -

CURIOSITY

Long before people could take pictures of Earth from out in space, they had figured out that Earth is a planet floating round and round our sun star as it, itself, spins through space. We had learned a lot of other things about Earth, and had a fairly good idea, from making globe maps, what it must look like if we could see the whole planet. But when the first astronauts actually brought back photos, people all over the world were amazed and delighted at Earth's shimmering beauty.

It looked like something more than a beautiful planet—like something alive and breathing as it whirls about! If you have seen videos of it as it spins, with its ever changing cloud patterns, you will be able to imagine it as a spinning dancer wrapped in misty white veils and see why the ancients saw her as the Greek goddess, Gaia.

The Greeks, as their language changed over time, called Gaia "Ge," which is the word from which we get our words geology, the study of Earth's formation; geometry, the measurement of Earth; and geography, the mapping of Earth. People have worked for a very long time on studies of Earth, such as geology, geometry, and geography, but they had hardly begun back when those ancient Greek villagers were listening to storytellers.

From the time we became human, our search for food and safe places to live—and sometimes just our curiosity—pushed us to take longer and longer trips. First people went only as far as their feet could carry them. Then they learned how to tame horses and make boats. Small boats had to stay near shores, so people invented bigger ones that could cross seas with the help of sails and oars. That was frightening when no one knew how big the seas were, because boats far out disappeared from sight as if they had fallen off the edge of the world.

This made people think that Earth was shaped something like a big pancake with the sea round its edge. We can imagine them happy and grateful each morning when the bright sun appeared overhead to light up the world. They were probably not so happy when the sun slipped down behind the edge of the world each evening, but at least there were little star lights and the moon to keep it from getting too dark. Some people, looking up at the moon, saw a face there and thought it was alive. Earth, too, felt alive to them, though they couldn't see its face because they were on it.

It was people's curiosity and search for new land that made them try to figure out the shape of Earth. But in their poetry and creation stories most of them saw Earth as the great Mother who gave them food and water, places to live and beautiful things to look at. We already know the ancient Greeks called her Gaia. Other peoples gave her different names, like Erda (from which the name Earth comes), Inana, or Matrona, but they were all names for Mother Earth or Mother Nature.

While some people were still living simple lives, respecting and loving nature, others got busy inventing new things—like those bigger and better ships that could venture further and further until they could cross whole oceans. Sailors reported that there was no edge to fall off, and soon mathematicians figured out that the world must be round as a ball. A librarian in ancient Alexandria, a few hundred years B.C., even figured out how big it is, though the knowledge that Earth was a great ball, and not a flat plate, was later lost for much over a thousand years and had to be rediscovered.

Now we are discovering that many ancient peoples, such as various Pacific island natives, Phoenicians, Greeks and Celts were crossing oceans, discovering new lands and people. As far as we can tell, they mostly traveled to each other's lands in peace and friendship, trading goods and sharing ideas. We do not know why such travels, in the Atlantic, at least, stopped around the time of the Roman Empire's fall, but we do know that Europeans lost even the memory of them until the time of Columbus.

In Columbus' time, there were stories of gold and other great riches in the far off land called India from which traders had brought spices and silks to Europe over land routes. Columbus, knowing the world was round, decided to find it by sailing the sea. The land route was a very long and difficult trip over endless mountains and deserts and through many dangers. He hoped that going in the opposite direction by sea one could sail around the world to get there more easily. Once his crew set out, dreams of gold kept them going.

What they found, as we all know, was the long forgotten land of America, but thinking it was India, they called the people they found there "Indians." Soon more Spanish expeditions were sent to seek gold, and where they found it, as among the Aztecs and Incas, they slaughtered people to get it. In most parts of America they found no gold, so they decided to take the land itself as well as silver and copper and things that could be grown. The Native American people they called Indians did not understand what was happening when these white men started dividing up the land, saying "This part is for our king, and this part is ours, and you will have to go and stay on that little piece over there." They thought it was very bad to cut the Great Mother Earth in pieces that way when she was here for all people to share and to love and to care for.

Meanwhile, in Europe, from which the white men had sailed, the old Nature religions in which people worshipped Earth were being suppressed by the Church. Many of the women who practiced this religion by doing ceremonies of gratitude and healing with natural herbs were burned at the stake as witches. Scientists, some of which were also punished by the Church for their ideas about Earth and the Universe, were nevertheless discovering interesting things. Their ideas began to make sense in terms of something new that Europeans were getting very excited about.

- 2 -

THE WORLD MACHINE

What the people in Europe were doing and getting excited about at that time was inventing machines—mechanical things made of iron and wood, nuts and bolts, wheels and other parts that moved. These machines could do work people had to do with their hands before, such as copying or printing books, spinning thread and weaving cloth.

Rich people, especially at the courts of kings, loved machines so much that they had special machines invented just to amuse themselves. Artists and engineers worked together, making mechanical music boxes, fancy clocks and jeweled wind-up birds to sing as nearly as possible like real ones.

At the same time, other scientists were trying to figure out how real birds and other animals worked. What made rivers flow and the weather change? How did the sun and planets and stars move through the sky around Earth?

There were many arguments about that question. The ancient Greek Aristarchos had said Earth moved around the sun, but Europeans, much as they respected the ancient Greeks, had been told by their priests that God had put Earth, the most important thing in the whole universe, right at the center, with everything else circling round it—the sun, the moon, the planets and all the stars.

With the help of new inventions such as the telescope, scientists finally proved that Earth is indeed a planet spiraling around its sun star as it moves through space. Its fellow planets were doing the same but were far enough from Earth to look like stars in the sun's reflected light, and our moon spiraled round Earth as other planets' moons did. They called all this the solar system, and later scientists understood that other stars could also be suns with their own planets spiraling around them. Some ancient peoples had known about the solar system in the distant past, but in Europe, it had to be rediscovered.

The wheeling patterns of the solar system and other stars made the scientists of that time think of clocks, with all their different-sized wheels going smoothly round and round. It was easier to think of the great spiraling patterns in the heavens as circles fixed in space like the wheels of a clock. So they built clocklike models of the universe and decided that was how it actually ran—like a gigantic well-oiled clock!

The biggest clocks on Earth were very large mechanisms built high on church steeples. Their great wheels turned each other not just to tell time, but to play music on the hour with puppets marching around in circles beating drums and playing horns while others brandished their swords. These life-size people puppets were mechanisms themselves. We could call them the first robots. No wonder people making such machines and seeing them work began thinking with pride that people could do practically anything with machines!

To the scientists who were trying to explain the universe, it seemed that the great clock of star and planet wheels might also have its robots. While Plato had seen God as a mathematician, Descartes, one of the leading founding fathers of European science, saw God more like an engineer, in that He created the world, including all its creatures, as mechanisms. This was a very exciting idea. Scientists are people with great curiosity about how things come to be and how they work, most eager to explain things. To them, the clockworks and robots idea was a way of explaining everything in the whole world, even in the whole universe! After all, men who invented machines could understand them completely, so it looked to them now that nature, which had appeared so mysterious, could finally be understood and explained. The scientists grew so sure of the world machine they had invented in their minds that they believed this was how nature had really been made.

Geologists began talking about geological mechanisms—how Earth was put together — and biologists began talking about the mechanisms of evolution—how plants and animals and people got invented by God the Engineer and just how they were put together from parts. Doctors spoke of heart and lung pumps and bone and muscle mechanisms, and early psychologists started talking about the machinery of the brain. They wanted to know how each of these mechanisms "ticked" and what went wrong with it when a person got sick.

Each kind of scientist had special kinds of mechanisms to study and explain. All together they were sure there would be no mysteries left in nature when each had explained their own part of it.

Scientists who study matter—the stuff the universe is made of —are called physicists. That's because they study what everything in nature is made of and the Greek word for nature is physis. Lots of scientific words come from the ancient languages of Greek and Latin. The ancient Greeks had had a lot of scientific ideas themselves, such as the one about Earth moving around the sun.

Another ancient Greek idea that interested physicists in Europe was that all nature is made of tiny bits of matter too small to see. The Greeks who thought of this had named them atoms from the word atomo, which means indivisible—the smallest things you cannot cut into pieces. Human society was made of individual people, the smallest parts of society that were not divisible, so the Greek word for individual, or person, was also atomo. Nature, too, they figured out, must be made of indivisible parts. Only natural atoms, unlike human ones, must be too small to see. They also reasoned that these natural atoms, unlike people, must all be alike.

Even though they were all alike, nature's atoms could form different kinds of matter, the ancient Greeks said. They could form stone or water, air or wood, or even living bodies, depending on the patterns in which the atoms were arranged. Even though the atoms were invisibly tiny, they must be so hard they could never be broken or destroyed. That meant atoms were not only the tiniest, but also the most lasting things of all. Even today, scientists believe that we are breathing in atoms today that were parts of ancient things and people.

More than two thousand years passed from the time the idea of atoms was born to the time when scientists had machines and mathematics that helped them prove atoms were really there as the invisibly tiny building blocks of every kind of matter. Physicists worked together with chemists, who study how atoms are put together, discovering that gases are made of floating atoms, liquids of slipping, sliding atoms, and solid things of atoms in stiffer patterns. It really began to look as if scientists had finally gotten down to the smallest parts of nature's wonderful machinery, and could now solve the mystery of all natural mechanisms.

But then it turned out they were in for a big surprise!

THE DANCE OF ATOMS

Actually, there were many surprises. First of all, atoms were not at all like tiny hard bits. Nor were they all alike.

Each atom seemed to be something more like a sun with planets spiraling around it—a tiny solar system. Because the whole thing was much too small to be seen even under a microscope, scientists had to guess its form from its behavior together with other atoms.

There was clearly something in the center, where the sun is in the solar system. They called it a nucleus and tried to figure out what the even tinier things whirling around it like planets could be. Different kinds of atoms seemed to have different numbers of these planet-things, which they called electrons. The nucleus was also different in different atoms. Some were clearly bigger and heavier than others, so they sorted them by 'atomic weights.'

The next surprise was that even the nucleus was made up of parts. More tiny bits, held together by forces so unbelievably strong that splitting the nucleus into its parts made an explosion. That discovery led to the making of atomic, or nuclear, weapons, and later to nuclear energy that could be turned into electricity.

Every atom, no matter how tightly locked into its place—as it is, for example, in a crystal—turns out to be a tiny mass of jiggling, whirling parts. All the parts, around the nucleus and inside it, are nowadays called particles. But even these particles aren't solid things.

That was the biggest surprise of all. The particles are like tiny whirling winds in a storm, or waves dancing on the sea. When physicists try to catch hold of them, they form, divide, disappear, turn into each other, do anything but hold still to be studied. All the physicists can describe, or try to describe, is the pattern of their dance with each other—a dance of pure energy, with nothing solid about it! Particles themselves, the very 'stuff' of matter, were actually energy.

What a headache for the physicists. Solid matter dissolves when you get right down to its tiniest parts. Fortunately, it doesn't dissolve into no-thing, for the pattern of the energy dance is always there to give matter its form. The only problem is that trying to separate the dancers from their dance to study them does not work. It's like trying to study a storm by taking a wave out of the sea, or a wind out of the air. Think about that for a moment—about a dance in which no step makes sense without the other steps being danced around it.

 The only way physicists can show us even a little of this dance is to break it up in such a way that they catch the pattern of its last steps. What they do is to hurl bunches of particles onto huge circle tracks, whipping up their speed as they go round and round the tracks, then finally crashing them into a target. This is done in giant machines called cyclotrons—the biggest machines in the world to study the tiniest things. Looking at the target afterwards, it shows the last traces of the tiny particle dancers dissolving or splitting, or flying off to look for new atoms to dance in. These traces are beautiful curves and spirals.

We may never be able to see the energy dance at its tiniest level the way it is when we don't disturb it, but we know for sure it is there—inside the stars and the seas and in our own bodies. Everything made of anything is made of this dance, and all the dances in the whole universe are woven into each other.

Next time you look at a rock or a chair, try to imagine the dance of which it is made. You may wonder why it doesn't fly apart and scatter all over the place. It has to be a very good dance not to do that—as if the dancers are all holding hands as they whirl and weave about, or are at least watching each other and keeping step so that the dance doesn't come apart. In a real dance of people, this would mean no one falling off the stage or confusing the others by bumbling.

Every piece of matter, everything we know, is a beautiful ballet made of countless invisible dancers' movements together. It is a dance too small to see, and yet so large it is the whole universe!

This reminded some physicists that ancient people in India had called the universe the dance of Shiva and his wife, Shakti. Shiva and Shakti were the names for the god and goddess who are forever creating and recreating the universe by dancing it into being. These ancient Indians, as well as the ancient Chinese and some other ancient cultures somehow knew what modern scientists have only recently learned: that while machinery is made of separate parts, the universe, or nature, cannot be taken apart. Dancers not dancing are not a dance—and the dance of living nature, of the whole universe, is All That Is.

Physicists everywhere now understand the universe this way, showing us that matter is a moving dance of energy forming endless patterns. What 'matters' is the design of the dance. People everywhere are getting this, too, that we are all One, all individually and together a single energy dance, all of us affecting each other's lives, all of us co-creating our dance now and always.

Perhaps the biggest question in science now is about the nature of this basic energy of All That Is. Just like the hunt for the tiniest indivisible 'original' particle from which all matter is composed, scientists now hunt for the original energy from which all the matter in the universe is made. Some physicists believe it is what we call consciousness as was, and still is, believed in the Vedic science of India; others disagree.

Because our eyes cannot see at microscopic levels, some dances in nature, such as those of rocks and mountains, appear to us to stay in the same positions for long periods of time. Others change their patterns gradually, if visibly, as in growing flowers and children. Many patterns are clearly changed around by each other, as when people build houses and then earthquakes destroy them.

Knowing all this about the universe and our world, we can see there is no great machine made of smaller mechanisms. The universe is much more like something truly alive—a great, magnificent dance in which everything has its role. Could it be that we and everything else in the universe are making up this dance as we go?

- 4 -
THE DANCE OF DNA

Physicists were not the only scientists in for surprises. Biologists, who study living things—'bio' coming from the Greek word for life, bios—also thought they were studying mechanisms to see how they worked.

After the microscope was invented, biologists saw that living things are made of tiny cells with walls around them. Inside the walls were tinier things they called organelles that appeared to float around in a kind of goo they called cytoplasm. There were two kinds of cells, some a very small kind we know as bacteria, and the others much larger, with a dark blob near their center. Those are called nucleated cells, because biologists called that central blob a nucleus just as physicists used that word for the center of the atom. Remember these two kinds of cells: tiny bacteria and much larger nucleated cells.

Later, when we talk about Earth as Gaia again, we will see that she herself may be a really gigantic cell on, in and over the surface of which tiny cells evolved. Seeing Earth from space as we now can, it is not too difficult to imagine her as a huge living cell. For now, let us just keep this in mind as we learn more about Earth's tiny cells.

All cells, of course, are much bigger than atoms, since they are made of atoms themselves. Groups of atoms stick together forming molecules, and the molecules in turn form chemicals of which cell parts are made. The most important kinds of molecules making up cells are proteins (think meat), lipids (think fat) and acids (think vinegar), especially DNA and RNA, which we will learn about shortly. Molecules, as big complexes of atoms, connect with each other to form the lively dance of the active chemical structures and activities in our cells. Every one of your nucleated cells is as complex as a large human city—a buzzing hive of amazing activities.

When Earth was still young, the earliest molecules hooked up in simple dances as they floated in seas and tossed in winds. Some such dances may have become the first cells when they were trapped in tiny fatty lipid bubbles at the edges of seas. Sunshine and rain wet and dried, heated and cooled, cracked and reformed the bubbles. Eventually they may have become Gaia's first single-cell creatures, the ancient bacteria that grew by feeding themselves on molecules of sugars and acids floating around them in the warm shallow coastal seas.

Their outer lipid walls bumped away the seawater in which they floated so it couldn't dissolve them—the way a drop of water on butter just rolls off it instead of soaking into it. They kept just enough water inside their cell walls so their own molecules could slide around doing their jobs. Most of the parts of cells were hard to see under ordinary microscopes, but biologists did discover something very important about the nucleus.

All cells can make more of themselves by splitting themselves into two. Biologists could see that before one of the larger nucleated cells divides, the nucleus itself splits into two parts. Unlike an atomic nucleus, which only splits by exploding, half the cell nucleus quietly moves away from the other half. Then the cell wall folds itself down between the two parts of the nucleus until each is enclosed by a wall, or sack, of its own, with its share of cytoplasm and other cell parts inside.

One cell thus becomes two. But there is something curious about these two new cells, for each of them has a nucleus just as big as the original one. How could the nucleus do this magical thing of dividing itself in half and having each half come out as big as the whole? Imagine pies dividing like that when we share them!

Scientists had seen that the nucleus was filled with dark lumps they called chromosomes. They suspected that chromosomes were the parts of cells that somehow carried the traits passed down to each of us from two long lines of ancestors that met in our parents, who passed their traits on to us—traits such as blue eyes, red hair, weak stomachs, artistic talents, intelligence and so on to all the things making us unique.

If these chromosomes were carrying those traits, they must be made of smaller parts biologists called genes even before they could see them. Just like the physicists they were trying to understand cells like machines by searching for their smallest parts and seeing how they were put together.

When the electron microscope was invented, microbiologists could see into cells more clearly and found that each chromosome lump was really a very long thread, very carefully wound up. Finally they figured out that each of these threads was something like a very long zipper, twisted round and round into a long spiral. Finally they had gotten right down to single molecules, for that's what each spiraling zipper was—a very long molecule made up of bunches of atoms strung together, a complex acid molecule they called DNA.

When a cell is about to divide, something peculiar happens to the DNA, though not so peculiar for zippers. It unzips! This splits the DNA molecules right down the middle. But, as with a real zipper, half a DNA zipper is no use at all.

In each half of the zipper, every little tooth that had been locked up with another tooth in the other half begins to act like a magnet. The zipper tooth begins to pull at other such 'teeth' floating around in the soupy cell until one sticks onto it. But the teeth are not all alike. They come in four kinds, and each one acts like a magnet only for those just like the old tooth partner it had.

We can picture this dance of the DNA zippers as if it were a dance that people did. If we do this, then the first zipper is a long double line made of couples. Each couple holds hands and stays in line behind the couple in front of it. Imagine that the dancers wear costumes in four different colors, so that there are green dancers, red dancers, blue dancers and yellow dancers. Green always dances with red, and blue always with yellow.

Now the partners let go hands one couple at a time, starting at the head of the line. The double line unzips itself like a zipper. But each half stays in line as the dance continues with two long strings of single dancers in green, red, blue and yellow costumes.

Imagine now that lots of single dancers dressed in the same four colors come onto the stage and dance around among the two lines of dancers. Every dancer in a line chooses a new partner from among the new dancers, always one wearing the same color as the old partner. When all the dancers in the two lines have chosen new partners, there are two double lines with just the same color pattern as the one with which the dance began.

In the real DNA dance, there are now two complete DNA molecules for every one with which we started out. So, all together, there are enough to wind up into two complete sets of chromosomes, or two complete nuclei—one for each of the two new cells to be formed. As the original cell divides, half its organelles go into each new cell and more of them are made until each new cell grows as big as the original.

As if that is not a miracle, think about this: In every one of your cells, the invisibly fine thread of DNA stretched out would be about two meters long. Remembering our dancers, there would be three billion (three thousand million) zipper teeth couples in each cell. The real DNA thread is much finer than the finest baby hair or spider silk you can even begin to imagine. Now, see the DNA in all your fifty to a hundred trillion cells stretched out into a single thread and imagine a jet pilot flying night and day along it. You may find this hard to believe, but that pilot would have to fly around ten thousand years to get to the end of your personal DNA!

In case you don't believe it, you, or someone you know good at math, can multiply the two meter pieces by your 50 to 100 trillion cells and divide by the normal jet speed of 500 kilometers per hour to see how many hours your pilot must fly. Then, work out the rest, but stop to remember that the hugely long thread the pilot is flying along is actually cut into those two-meter pieces stuffed into the invisibly small nucleus in each of your cells along with proteins and water! Isn't it awesome that something as tiny as a cell can be so fantastically complex? Wait till we get to know its organelles!

If the DNA carries our traits, then it is clearly important to copy it exactly in every cell division. Otherwise we could not remain our very individual selves as we grew from a single egg cell that kept dividing from 2 to 4 to 8 to 16 to 32 to 64 and so on up to our 50 to 100 trillion cells! Nor could we pass on the traits we inherited to our children.

But DNA cannot just copy itself as was believed. The real story is much more complex and fascinating. To understand the role of DNA we have to talk about another kind of molecule called protein.

When you look into a mirror you are pretty much seeing protein. Skin, hair, eyes, muscle, blood, nerves, parts of bones and your inner organs are all made of cells and cells are made mostly of proteins, though some can store a lot of inactive fat. Another way to look at this is that, after water and fat, there are more proteins than anything else in your body.

Biologists estimate there are around 50,000 different kinds of protein molecules in our cells. DNA turned out to be the magical molecule that contains the instructions, or code, for making all those proteins. We call the lengths of DNA that code for each kind of protein genes. Remember the dancers? The patterns of their colors down their lines represent instructions for building proteins. Each gene is a unique DNA 'dancer sequence' coding for a particular kind of protein.

It turns out that it is actually proteins that wrap and unwrap the DNA molecules to pack them into chromosomes and then to unwind them and unzip them when it is time to divide. Specialized proteins in the cell must find the right genes for making particular proteins needed by the cell and copy the information to make them. Without proteins, DNA would be quite useless as it cannot move on its own—kind of like a library with stacks of books full of useful information but no one to read them and put them to use.

At the time biologists were still figuring out just what DNA is, computers were the hot new technology. Soon biologists were talking about DNA as the cell's central computer that is somehow programmed to run the whole cell. Biologists, like physicists, are trained to use this kind of machine language. So, as the role of proteins became increasingly clear, they were seen as 'molecular machinery' carrying out the commands of the nuclear computer.

In seeing life as a dance, rather than as machinery, it seems more helpful to see DNA as a library in which the books must be read and used to get things done. The many kinds of proteins in a cell appear to know and tell each other just what needs to be done where and when. Think of them as having social networks. They share information with the kinds of proteins that can hunt for the 'gene books' and copy them onto RNA molecules that are shorter and simpler versions of DNA. The RNA is then taken by proteins to other proteins which are assembled into organelles called ribosomes that can build new proteins from the RNA pattern.

DNA and protein molecules do the dance of life together. DNA stores information the way recipes and blueprints do—information certain proteins use to make the huge number of different kinds of proteins in every cell. Every kind of plant and animal has its own special pattern of DNA, its own set of instructions, duplicated in each of its cells as they divide, starting with the original seed or egg and ending up as a whole plant or animal. Once biologists could tell one set of genes from another, they could tell one species of creature from another. That is how we know for sure that a rose is not a lily and a cat is not a dog.

As proteins do all of the cell's work, they get damaged or wear out and must be replaced. If you have ever seen a chipper machine that grinds up dead trees into chips, imagine one in which a living tree came out at the end instead of dead chips! That is difficult to imagine, isn't it? Well, that is exactly the kind of thing that happens in your cells. The useless proteins are recycled into brand new healthy proteins day and night by pulling them into protein recycling centers—around 20,000 per cell—taking them apart and weaving their parts into new living wholes. How do the proteins that are organized into such centers know which other proteins to recycle and how to do that?

It usually takes several different kinds of proteins for any given task. The more scientists learn about proteins the more they seem to be the smart molecules of nature, perhaps even smart enough to have invented DNA in the first place! It would have been very useful for them, after all, to have libraries of information for reproducing themselves, since they have to rebuild each other from scratch, being unable to divide like cells.

Scientists can identify and map the kinds of atoms in protein molecules and the way they are linked into chains and folded into complex patterns. They can also track the complex activities of proteins in cells, and even see that they 'talk' to each other, but they still do not have a clue how proteins know what to do and when and how to do it. Nor, for that matter, do they know what most of our DNA is for. All the protein-coding genes scientists have found add up to less than five percent of the DNA in our cells. They know little about the other 95% of our DNA. Fortunately, we don't have to know how it all works, because our proteins do know everything needed about our DNA to rebuild and run our cells, keeping them healthy!

- 5 -
THE DANCE OF CELL ORGANELLES

The cell's organelles outside the nucleus were thought to be mechanisms programmed by the nuclear computer as it turned them on or off and made them do jobs like making energy from food, building new parts, cleaning up wastes or carrying supplies around and getting the cell ready to divide. Surely they were very efficient little machines. But

then biologists discovered something strange that did not fit this machine picture very well.

Some of the little 'machines' around the nucleus have their own DNA. It is different from the DNA in the nucleus by which our human species is identified. Yet it is very like some other kinds of DNA biologists knew about. They had found it in some tiny bacteria that were very like the first bacteria we learned about earlier as Earth's very first creatures billions of years ago.

Now if those little 'machines have their own DNA instructions, then they must be creatures themselves. In fact, it seems they are the direct descendants of ancient bacteria that have been making more of themselves for billions of years with hardly any mistakes. What's more, they live in the cells of every kind of creature made of nucleated cells—in funguses, plants, animals and us. It's high time we knew them by name. They are mitochondria, which comes from the Greek words meaning 'thread-grains' because under the microscope they look like tiny grains filled with thread.

What on Earth are all those mitochondria doing inside us? They are keeping us alive!

That is the most amazing thing about them. Without them we couldn't lift a finger. If they left us, we'd die. One biologist, Lewis Thomas, the first to see Earth as a giant cell, laughed at the old machinery of life ideas. He said that the mitochondria are neither machines nor machine parts; that if anything in nature is a machine, maybe it's us. He suggested we could be giant taxis the ancient bacteria built to get around in safely. That may not be as crazy as it sounds, because later we will see that they actually did invent electric motors!

Certainly they've done very well multiplying themselves throughout the living world almost from the beginning of it. There are on average a thousand mitochondria in each of our cells. All together they may make up almost half our weight—and half that of elephants and insects, clams and monkeys, lizards and fish and worms. That means a big part of all of us different multi-celled creatures is made of the same kind of very ancient microbes. Living things too small to see without microscopes, including bacteria, viruses and single nucleated cells, are called microbes.

You must be wondering how it is that mitochondria can keep us alive, so that we couldn't get along without them. From the earliest times, they have been the experts at making the energy that keeps creatures growing and going. They make it inside us from the food we eat and the air we breathe. Swarms of these friendly little mitochondria work day and night at this job, never resting.

Actually we could call them our cell's bankers. Have you ever heard anyone say, "Money is energy?" Well, the mitochondria actually package the energy into molecules called ATP (for adenosine triphosphate) and send them out all over the cell wherever energy is needed. ATP molecules are like stored value debit cards—bank cards pre-loaded with spendable money. Worker proteins called catalysts are given these cards to catalyze (make happen) all the cell's activities.

When they have spent the energy money loaded onto the cards, they take them back to the bankers to get them reloaded. They never have to pay back the money, much less interest. The mitochondria banks simply issue just the right amount of ATP money as is needed to make the cell's economy run smoothly. What if we humans had such a free money system with banks there to issue and regulate it without getting people into debt? Many alternative currency systems (easy to Google these three words) are testing such systems successfully.

In plants—from seaweed to daisies to potatoes and oak trees – mitochondria live together with some ancient relatives of theirs called chloroplasts. The chloroplasts, also descended from ancient bacteria, are experts at making energy from sunlight and are what give plants their green color. They feed on carbon dioxide gas (CO2) to make ATP energy and give off oxygen as a waste gas. Now oxygen is just what mitochondria need to make their ATP energy money as they give off carbon dioxide. The two thus work very well together.

 Plants and single-celled creatures containing chloroplasts thus produce oxygen while the mitochondria of all creatures release carbon dioxide. That is how Earth's air, containing both gases, nourishes the very life that produced them. This cooperative dance, which we'll learn more about later, makes chloroplasts and mitochondria the most important beings on Earth, although they are the tiniest and most invisible.

Ever since they were discovered by the first scientists to look through microscopes, people have thought of microbes as things that make us sick.   Actually most microbes are very friendly and helpful.

 Each of us is not so much a single being as a great colony of cooperating microbes. We still don't know how many kinds live in us. Besides the mitochondria in our cells, there are friendly bacteria all over our skins and in our guts. Scientists are starting to count them all as necessary parts of us because they are learning more and more about why we could not live without them.

Our gut bacteria digest our food and protect us from whatever harmful bacteria and viruses get into us by running most of our immune system. We need to pay far more attention to feeding them healthy nourishing foods instead of stressing them out dealing with junk food!

If you were as tiny as mitochondria are and could peek inside any of your cells, you would hear them humming and clicking and tapping out the rhythms of their energy-making dance. You would see the exchange of supplies, wastes and information from other cells moving through passageways in each cell's wall. You know now that there may be a thousand bankers in any particular cell along with twenty thousand recycling centers, so you can more easily imagine each cell as a large human city.

Hundreds of thousands of things are happening in each of your city-cells every second of every day even while you are asleep. Unlike machinery, life never stops to rest. And unlike machinery, our proteins, including the DNA book readers, the bankers and the recyclers, are not created and run by intelligent machine engineers or computer programmers, but are intelligent themselves!

Remember the beautiful dances inside and among atoms, then inside and among molecules, and now among organelles within cells and with other microbes living in and on us. This dance, as we will see, is woven together all over our planet and most likely on countless other planets around the universe. The very same DNA information found in our cells has been exchanged among all microbes, funguses plants and animals all over our beautiful Earth throughout its life, always with the help of intelligent proteins!

Next we will look at how this dance of life came to be. In order to tell that story, we'll have to go back all the way to before Earth existed. Or, as the ancient Greek storyteller said, back to the time before Gaia's dance began, when there was a great No-thing.

- 6 -

HOW GAIA'S DANCE CAME TO BE

When the ancient storyteller called the beginning of the universe "a great no-thing," he would also have called it "the great All That Is." How can anything be nothing and all that is at once? Surely, this sounds like a riddle. But our storyteller understood that when nothing existed yet, there was the possibility for all things to come into being. That is why the ancient Greeks called the original universe chaos, meaning the possibility of everything in no-thing. Once things did come into being, the universe was called cosmos, meaning the pattern of All That Is.

Exactly how the very first things came into being will probably always be something of a mystery to us—too great and wonderful for us to understand completely. Even scientists, when they try to explain the beginnings of things seem to talk in riddles. Many of them nowadays believe that the universe began with an unimaginably huge explosion of energy from a single point. And yet they say this point was everywhere in the universe at once. Such riddles come up because the time and space by which we tell when and where things happen did not exist when the universe began.

Most scientists believe that the universe happened with a single Big Bang of energy. More and more of them believe it began as gentler ripples of energy in an endless energy field or sea. All of them agree that the universe is made of energy, so let us begin with that.

One way to think of energy is as a keyboard on which the highest keys are the energy we cannot see, but clearly experience and call by names such as consciousness, spirit or mind. In the middle range of keys that energy has slowed down to what is called electromagnetic energy, some of which we can see as light and color. In the low keys, as Einstein showed us, the energy has slowed down to where we can see and feel it as matter—stuff so dense we can sit on it and stub our toes on it.

Think of yourself as being, and playing on, this entire keyboard of matter, energy, spirit the way a dancer and a dance are one. There is no dance without a dancer and no dancer without a dance. Just so, you are a matter-energy-spirit being and the dance of your life all in one.

If the whole universe is, like ourselves, a keyboard of energy, we can more easily see why the physicists looking for the very smallest indivisible things in the universe discovered that their particles turned out to be dances of pure energy and not solid at all. It was as if what they were hunting for in the low keys turned out to have its source up in the highest keys!

 The important thing is to understand that the particle dance inside the atoms that combine to make molecules and all the bigger energy dances of our familiar world are part of an even greater universal dance. The steps of this dance up and down the keyboard grew into more and more complex and beautiful patterns as it evolved.

Evolution is the word we use for the way a dance we make up changes over time, just as biologists use the same word to describe the changes in Earth and its creatures over time. That is exactly why this book tells the story of Earth's evolution as a great dance.

We already know the tiniest particles team up with each other into the patterns we know as the simplest of atoms. So we understand how matter is actually pure energy. The simplest atoms of the early universe swirled around as great clouds of gas, sparking with light as the dancers bumped into each other.

The energy of each dancer combined with great universal forces we call radiation that moves outward to fly things apart and gravitation that pulls things together. These forces pulled the particles into tightly dancing atoms or scattered them widely. Between them, radiation and gravitation formed the clouds of gas atoms into beautiful swirling patterns—the beginnings of galaxies.

Notice that radiation is the word we use to describe light. We speak of the sun's rays moving outward from it. Radiation is the outward movement of the energy dance. When it is too weak to see with our eyes we can still feel it as heat, such as from radiators and from each other.

Because telescopes only show us radiating energy, such as starlight, they can only show us the outward movement, or expansion, of our universe.   We   know   its   invisible   inward   movement—its 'magnetism'—as gravitation. Gravitation is never seen but clearly felt. We feel Earth's gravitational pull on us as our own weight. The word 'magnetism' usually means that pulling force when strongly felt, but real magnets usually have two poles, like Earth, thus combing the outward and inward forces of expansion and attraction or contraction.

Electromagnetism, EM for short was first known from natural events such as lightning. Lightning   forms from the inward collisions of electron particle dancers that is strong enough to create the outward explosion of light. Capturing this dance and controlling it gave us electricity, which was useful for so many things it changed people's whole way of life.

If ancient people could have seen new galaxies forming—as we can today through our powerful telescopes—they would have called this the beginning of Gaia's dance, the first view of the spiraling veils from which stars and then planets would form. We can only wonder how they knew of these patterns without having telescopes.

Inside these spiraling veils of gas, the force of gravitation pulled many atoms more and more tightly together. They began forming loose balls, just as the dust under beds does when breezes stir it up. In the center of such balls the atoms bumped into each other so hard that it got very hot from all the pushing and shoving. These great balls got heavier and heavier, beginning to glow from all the heat inside them. So the giant gas balls became stars!

Great galaxies formed, sparkling with countless stars of different sizes. Every star we see in our own sky at night is inside our own galaxy, called the Milky Way, from the Greek word for milky, galaxis. We can see only a small number of all the Milky Way's stars. Far beyond them are other galaxies full of stars, and all the galaxies in the universe dance together in patterns, just as particles dance inside atoms.

The dances of particles and atoms, galaxies and galactic clusters, are the smallest and largest dance patterns we know. In their interactions, they weave each other into new patterns of in-between sizes, such as our Earth and our selves. Ancient people somehow got this in saying, "As above, so below."

When the inside of a star becomes a real frenzy—like a very crowded dance floor when the music is fast and loud—the jammed-up atoms are crushed into larger, heavier, new types of atoms. Each kind of atom is called an element and has a unique pattern of particles in and around its nucleus as we saw in describing the dance of atoms. Eventually whole stars may explode from all the pressure, shooting their atoms, old and new, out into space as gas and heavier dust. The exploding stars are called supernovas. Their gases swirl into new young stars and gaseous planets around them while their dust may form into smaller, heavier balls of matter as solid planets. The force of gravitation holds planets in their paths around the new stars formed from a supernova explosion.

Our own planet Earth almost surely formed, along with the rest of the solar system, after such an explosion around five billion years ago. One way we can tell this is that some of the tiny atoms all over Earth, even in our bodies, are still exploding. These micro-explosions are actually left over from the supernova that gave birth to our solar system, though they are much too small for us to see, feel or notice at all.

Most of the atoms that were formed in stars that exploded as supernovas are stable , but some, such as some types of potassium, are unstable and keep on 'exploding' as what we call radioactivity for billions of years. Atoms of this radiopotassium in your body explode approximately 12,000 times every second. This actually makes your body radioactive and a small percentage of cancers may arise from these explosions, but on the whole they cause no problems because they are so tiny and there are no chain reactions among them to make them dangerous

Most atoms in us are much more stable, despite the lively dance going on inside them, but all of them came from the stars. Without stars we would never have come to be. Stardust is not just fairytale magic; it is what we are really made of!

New stars are formed, grow and change as they get older, then finally die. Some just burn out, collapse and grow cold. Others explode, scattering their matter into space like seeds from a bursting pod, forming whole new stars and planets in their turn as we just saw. Astronomers who study the stars are seeing that the dance of the stars is as real as the dance of the atoms, and they speak more and more of the "lives" of stars, rather than the machinery of the universe.

The more we learn about such things, the less the universe seems like a giant machine and the more it seems to be alive as a whole, creating and caring for itself.

It seems we are learning to explain scientifically things people knew as stories from ancient times. In the myth of Gaia's dance, you will recall, she just whirled round and round in space at first. Her dancing created the seas as sweat from her body and then the sky of air before she gave birth to forests and animals and people. It turned out, as scientists discovered, that Earth did come to life as a whirling planet body creating its own seas and atmosphere and creatures.

Some of the dust from the supernova that gave birth to the solar system gathered into an Earth-ball that gradually grew heavier and spun around faster. The heat of pressure kept most of it a molten fiery liquid called magma that flows around a heavier solid metal core of iron and nickel. It now seems this core contains enormous iron crystals that would look like giant trees packed together. The lightest minerals of all, such as silicon, floated to the surface.

 The core and the liquid magma around it together produce a great EM (electromagnetic) field around Earth. This field of energy is its own special dance, made of electron particle dancers like those we found in atoms, but now doing their own dance by themselves, flowing in huge ring-like and spiraling patterns around our planet. This field is good for Earth as it traps particles from the sun's 'solar wind' that would otherwise strike Earth causing damage. It also gives us our north/south compass directions for birds and people to navigate by. Sometimes we see this EM field energy dance as beautiful auroras.

Within this field, Earth's surface touches cold space, and so the hot young planet grew a thin crusty skin, a bit the way homemade pudding forms a skin as it cools, or fat hardens on top of cooling gravy. On Earth this skin got as hard as rock, for that's just what it was, a crust of rock around the hot core and fiery liquid magma.

As Earth whirled around, this thin crust cracked open in places, letting the molten magma inside ooze out as lava. With the pressure on it suddenly released in its escape, the lava separated itself into heavy atoms that cooled into more rock, water made of gas atoms—hydrogen and oxygen joining into H20 water molecules—and loose gas atoms and molecules light enough to float away from the surface of the planet. Those that did not escape formed its atmosphere.

Steamy water vapor piled up around the young Earth and cooled to form heavy clouds. These rained down huge quantities of water, much of which stayed on the surface and began covering the heavier rock. Ice brought in by comets added to Earth's water supply as more and more surface cracks released lava so the crust grew thicker and thicker with hardening rock.

Meanwhile the clouds continued to gather, the comets kept coming and the seas grew deeper and deeper. The Sun and Earth between them also created electrical storms among the clouds, making the pattern of weather more complex. Thus the EM energy dance continued everywhere from the insides of atoms to Earth's great fields and the sun itself.

The sun's EM flowing to the young whirling Earth met the EM coming from the inside of Earth, stirring up new dance patterns on its surface. The same EM that holds the outer particle dancers of atoms into orbit around the nucleus could now stir up loose gas and dust atoms on the surface of the new planet. This dance of matter and energy together created new molecular partnerships. It was the beginning of a chemistry that later led to forming creatures, though that was still a long way off.

As Earth's crust grew thicker and lumpier, new streams of lava broke through it with greater force. Volcanoes, shooting their fiery insides high into the air , formed mountains as their lava cooled and hot ashes settled down. Other mountains were formed when earthquakes cracked the crust and slid parts of it over each other, or from the heaving of the crust where the insides pushed but did not break.

Sliding rocks were ground into sand, and rivers of rainwater running over exposed rocks wore grooves into them, washing sand down to the seas. The rivers also carried along salts and minerals from the rocks themselves. As they were swept into the seas, the seas became salty.

The light gases floating around the planet were not like the air we breathe now. They were thin and of a different mixture, probably rather like the atmospheres of some planets that never came to life, or at least did not stay alive, such as Venus and Mars.

If we could watch this early part of Earth's history as a movie we ran very fast, it would look like the dance of a living being trying hard to express itself. We would see it whirling and heaving and sighing bursts of steam. We would see its skin lifting and falling and sliding about. It would be wounded by flying meteors from space, and might seem to be bleeding the red-hot lava from its torn skin. But always it would heal itself, and slowly it would become bluer with its gathering seas under an even thicker veil of white clouds.

Sunlight falling on it would make it shimmer and glow bright against the darkness of space until it began to look like the photos that astronauts can take of it now. And as some astronauts have said, when you see it from afar it is very hard not to believe that Earth is alive.

Of course it took many millions of years for even this much to happen, and no one was around to take movies. But we can use our imaginations, together with what we know, to create our own images of these beginnings.

The ancient Greek myth of Gaia began with an image of the goddess whirling out of darkness, wrapped in floating veils. Other ancient cultures had similar images of cosmic beginnings, such as the Indian one of a goddess stirring up whirls in a sea of milk. Many early images contained this basic pattern of a great whirling spiral. It is amazing that many ancient peoples were able to sense that the universe is a single dance of energy from which all things and creatures of the world came to be. Modern science took a long time to discover the same reality.

If our Greek storyteller of three thousand years ago came back to life and learned all we know now, he would not have to change his story very much. Gaia, expressing herself as Earth, would form the mountains and seas from her spinning body just as he said long ago.

It was not easy for Earth to make the air we breathe now as we will soon see. None of the other planets in our solar system have created seas and air and living creatures as Earth has. It is clear to us now that few planets among many can create such abundant life. Of course we continue to search for life on some moons in our own solar system and out among the stars. The universe is so huge and has so many stars and planets, that a "few" living planets could be billions!

Mars and Venus, the nearest planets to ours, may have tried and failed to develop life. It takes a great deal of work and cooperation to make a living planet a success. To form and grow living creatures a planet must have mobile materials, such as magma, water and atmospheric gases to circulate and recycle supplies. It must also be the right distance from its star so that its temperature will be right for life. James Lovelock, the scientist who showed us that Earth is alive, and called our living Earth 'Gaia', pointed out that that Venus was too hot and Mars too cold, while Earth was just right for life. He called it the "Goldilocks effect."

The tiniest dances in atoms are interwoven with the great dances of galaxies out in space. Just so, living creatures can only evolve on planets where the dances of the smallest and largest things are in step with each other.

Scientists have traced Earth's plants and animals, and the cells they are made of, all the way down to atoms and particles inside atoms. They thought when they understood all this that they would know just how life happened. But it wasn't enough.

It wasn't enough because they had not looked very much at the large dance patterns of Earth – at how the dance of living creatures is woven together with the great dance of Earth itself: Gaia's Dance.

Some of the things we now know about Earth seem magical. One of them is that the temperature of Earth seems hardly to have changed while the sun has gotten very much hotter since Earth was formed. Minor changes in her temperature have caused ice ages and hot ages, which seem extreme to us humans but are really only a difference of 6 to 8 degrees from what we call normal. To Gaia they were just brief chills and fevers from which she recovered.

How can Earth keep a constant temperature and recover easily if it is disturbed a few degrees? The only thing we know that can keep its temperature the same, except for the odd chill or fever, no matter what goes on around it, is a living body.

Since we discovered and harnessed electricity, we have created a global industrial society fueled by ancient oil Gaia had kept safely underground. Coal and oil are the tightly squeezed remains of ancient forests and dinosaurs and other creatures pushed underground as new life evolved on the surface. Digging up coal and pumping oil from the ground and then burning them to make electricity has now caused a lot of pollution and disturbed the balance of our atmosphere and seas dangerously.

In just a few hundred years—a very short time in Gaia's billions of years of life—we have burned so much coal and oil that we are giving Gaia a hot age fever. We humans have never had to survive one of those because we weren't around when the last one happened. The polar ice at both poles and our mountain glaciers are all melting away rapidly now and our best scientists and engineers cannot stop it from happening as long as we keep burning all that coal and oil. We will talk more about this later.

We have learned that a little more or less salt in the seas, or a little more or less oxygen in the air, would make it impossible for life as it is now to exist. There are always things going on to disturb and change this exact amount of salt and oxygen, yet somehow—at least until now—it has always stayed the same. This, too, is like what goes on in our own bodies, where the salt and oxygen in our blood and other cells are always kept in exactly the right balance to keep us alive and healthy.

Just as our blood flows round and round in our body, water and gases flow round and round in and on the body of Gaia. We can see part of the water flow as rain coming down, flowing into rivers and seas, rising up again as clouds. What we cannot see is that trees pump much water from the soil up into the sky through their roots, trunks and leaves. Meanwhile, vast numbers of mostly invisible tiny creatures called plankton floating on the seas help to make the clouds form overhead as well.

Do you know that even a thunderstorm looks like a living creature? It walks along on one big foot like a clam or a snail, except its foot is made of hard, cool rain. Its head is icy with hail. As warm air rises around it, it feels its way along, gliding over the ground and eating up clouds as it goes. All around its edges, it makes smaller storms, like children, before it dies. And of course its rain gives all of us life.

We cannot see the gases in our air flowing, as they are invisible. But we know that countless tiny mitochondria, chloroplasts and free-living bacteria not part of cells, as well as other creatures, are constantly busy changing the gases around and keeping them in the right balance.

Just as our bodies have the knowledge and wisdom to keep themselves going and to take care of themselves, so does the larger body of Gaia that we are all part of. This is the larger dance we are just beginning to understand. The dance of tiny things cannot be understood without looking at the larger dance, and the large dance can only be understood by knowing about the smaller dance.

Let us hope that we will wake up quickly to the dangers we are creating and bring our human dance back into step with our mother planet, Gaia.

7

Gaia's Problems

It's hard to say just what kind of living being Gaia is, because we have not yet found any other like her, and because we are just getting to know her. From the astronauts' photos of her we see she is beautiful beyond our earlier dreams. From scientists' discoveries about her we see she has wisdom, intelligence and love in some sense of what these words mean. Of course she is not a human being, much less a goddess, though such images help our imaginations just as they did in ancient myths.

One scientist, as we said, suggested she is something like a giant cell, a single-celled creature, because she is round and her atmosphere skin lets energy in and out like a cell wall. Yet no cell has fiery hot insides. She is not like any other being we know—she is our one and only living Earth, Gaia.

Whatever we believe she is, it is clear that we are part of her dance of life. It is also becoming clear that she has given us people the special task of using our minds to understand how she cares for us, and how we must cooperate in caring for her.

Now that we know how Gaia began her dance as our planet Earth, spiraling around our sun, let's see what she did next. So far, her surface is made of rock and sand, rivers and seas, clouds and rain and thin gases. She is full of her own core energy that generates a huge magnetic field. That interacts with the sun's energy as all sorts of molecules form on Gaia's skin to begin a new movement in the great dance of life. But starting a really good new dance is never easy, and Gaia had some very tough problems to solve.

One of these problems was the constant shower of meteors crashing into her. Every day these space rocks of all sizes came hurtling at her, striking and wounding her. If she hadn't found a way to protect herself, she might well have ended up as lifeless and pockmarked by meteor craters as is our moon.

Another problem was that while she needed our sun's energy to help her make living creatures, there was a bit too much of it for living creatures to stand. Gaia's first creatures, we already know, were bacteria. Because bacteria still live all over Earth now, this ancient kind was called archebacteria, meaning ancient bacteria and pronounced 'arki-bacteria.' Bacteria and nucleated cells such as ours were long thought to be the only two kinds of cells ever to evolve.

Then, not long ago, biologists discovered a third kind of cell in that primeval world of early Gaian life. They called these cells archaea because they did not seem to be bacteria. Nor were they nucleated cells. They were somewhere in between, small as bacteria, but with more organized DNA than bacteria had, along with a few other distinguishing features.

It appears that these archaea contributed to forming the nucleus in the big nucleated cooperatives, while actual bacteria became their chloroplasts and mitochondria. In this book, to keep things as simple as possible, we will consider the archaea as still belonging to the archebacteria, which we will call archebacs from now on for short.

Archebacs in that primeval world had to find places and ways to develop in safety from the burning part of sunlight we call ultraviolet rays. Some ultraviolet is good for life, but too much burns it badly, as you know if you have ever been sunburned.

The safest place was inside the seas just deep enough for the water to filter out the dangerous rays. But Gaia also had other good reason for starting living things in the sea—they needed water to form themselves and move about in.

For thousands of millions of years, the tiny bubbles or bags of molecules that evolved into archebacs tried out new arrangements and ways of life as they kept making more of themselves. The shallow edges of seas warmed by the sun, and places around deep sea hot springs became a rich bacterial soup.

We usually hear about bacteria as things that make us sick, but very few of them ever cause us such trouble, as we saw earlier. They are really the most marvelous creatures of all, because they were the first to figure out the problems of living and we still couldn't get along without them. Certainly Gaia couldn't get along in her dance of life without them. They were the first children in her dance, very eager to explore the possibilities of living, very eager to try out new things.

Most archea made their energy by swallowing up smaller things such as molecules of sugars and acids they found floating around them. Archebacs were so successful that they filled the seas and land and even the air until they were actually in danger of dying out because they were eating up the free sugars and acids faster than they could be replaced. Their great success had caused a great problem: global hunger!

As the food molecules ran short, some bacteria facing this problem got very clever. They invented a new way of making a living directly from the energy of sunlight. Perhaps you can guess that they are the very ones whose much later descendants became the chloroplasts of plants. If you did you will recall that they let out oxygen gas, which they made along with needed energy by using a green chemical called chlorophyll.

Unfortunately, this oxygen gas was very poisonous to other kinds of early bacteria. This is because oxygen is a deadly gas that destroys many kinds of molecules. Oxygen makes metals rust and fires burn. At first it was absorbed into the waters and rocks of Earth, but eventually it piled up in the atmosphere and many archebacs died of it. Thus a second global crisis was caused by archebacs: global pollution.

How fascinating that the archebacs caused the same kinds of global problems that we are causing now! No other creatures of Earth evolving between them and us have done this, so we will come back to this strange similarity later in our story.

Poor Gaia! The dangerous new oxygen gas was killing off many of her first children, while she herself faced the challenge of meteors, and of the ultraviolet rays that made it hard to keep her creatures alive. Danger, however, is a challenge to living things and the archea began working on solutions to the oxygen pollution. Eventually, Gaia's larger dance and the dance of her tiniest creatures together turned the oxygen crisis into a solution for all these problems!

When a molecule is broken up, the energy of its atoms is freed and can be used in other ways. This is just how some of the bacteria had been getting their energy—by breaking up those sugar and acid molecules they found in the seas. If they could protect their own molecules from being broken up by the oxygen and use it instead to break up food molecules, they might have a new and better way of getting their energy from food.

That's exactly what they learned to do. While the bluegreen bacteria continued making their energy and oxygen from sunlight and carbon dioxide gas, another kind of bacteria began making their energy by using the oxygen to break up food molecules. As they did so, they produced carbon dioxide as their waste gas. Just what the bluegreen bacteria needed. What a great way to cooperate!

Meanwhile, other bacteria that were harmed by the oxygen just dug themselves down into the soft mud on the sea bottom or packed themselves together in mats of clay that oxygen couldn't get into. Some of their kind survive even today, always looking for places safe from oxygen, such as muddy swamps or cow guts, where they help digest food the cows eat, and even our own guts where they do all sorts of good things for us as we will see later.

Many kinds of bacteria began spreading out onto land along the shores and then moved steadily over the rocks, often sticking together in patches or mats as they went. Some were blown through the air to land in new places.

Life was safer and ever more oxygen was made. So much that the oxygen-users couldn't begin to use it all, and it still floated upwards into the atmosphere. As the atmosphere got thicker, it was harder for meteors to get through it. A blanket of air seems very thin to us. We can just barely feel it by waving our arms around in it. But what we feel against our arms would be much harder if our arms waved much faster. After all, it is air that holds up fast-moving airplanes.

 Meteors move so fast that the air is quite solid to them. Rubbing hard against a solid thing produces heat, as you can feel by rubbing your hand against a table. Meteors rub up against the air so fast it burns them up. When we see their fiery tracks at night, high in the sky, we call them shooting stars, though they are really just burning rocks.

So, the dangerous oxygen had become a solution to another problem—the meteor problem. Once the atmosphere was thick with oxygen, very few meteors were heavy enough to land on Earth before they burned up.

That left only the problem of the ultraviolet rays. Some of the bacteria had learned to protect themselves with shields, something like the way we protect our eyes from strong light with sunglasses, and our skins with sun lotions. But many were still in danger. Once again oxygen came to the rescue.

Oxygen gas is made of twin oxygen atoms dancing together as molecules. As the ultraviolet rays struck these molecules in the air, it often broke them up. But the separated twins were often able to join other pairs to form triplet molecules. Triplet molecules make a different gas called ozone. A whole layer of this ozone formed in the middle of the atmosphere and the ultraviolet rays found it difficult to get through. Now there were far fewer of them getting down to Earth's surface, and life got even safer.

Gaia's children were safely living off each other's waste gases and multiplying in the seas and on the land. The great problems of meteors and ultraviolet rays no longer stood in her way.

While some scientists see Earth now as Gaia, many other scientists still think it is better to try and explain the world as complex machinery, and not as a living planet. But a mechanism is actually very different from an organism, so let's look at how that is so.

People have always designed machines to copy things other living beings do. Spinning and weaving machines copy spiders. Pumps copy hearts or the way trees pump water from the ground high up to their leaves. Airplanes copy birds in flight and submarines copy fishes and dolphins. Computers are our way of trying to copy what our brains can do. But life will always do more than our machines in some important ways.

An easy way to see a big difference between machines and living things is this: if you go way from one of your machines, such as your computer or iPhone for a while, you had better hope it does not change while you are gone. Even a small change would probably mean it was broken. But if you leave a living thing, such as your cat or your brother for a time, you had better hope they keep on changing, for if they don't, they will die.

A machine is created from the outside by someone who puts its pieces together in just the right way to make it do what is wanted. But a living being creates itself from an egg or a seed and keeps renewing its parts continually as we saw going on in our cells. When something goes wrong with a machine, a human must repair it, while a living being can often repair itself.

Earth, as Gaia, created herself within the larger dance of the universe, about which we know very little as yet. A new baby creates itself within the body of its mother. All Gaia's creatures from archebacs to us created ourselves within her body, using other creatures, plant and animal, to grow ourselves.

One ancient Greek philosopher named Anaximander said, "Everything that forms in nature incurs a debt, which it must repay so that other things may form." If you think about that, it is a whole story of evolution in just one sentence. Life recycles life to keep itself going, and as it does that, generation after generation, it also changes its dance of evolution. That is why new species appear in the dance while others die out.

Without our parents we cannot create ourselves, and without their care we could not survive. Without them we would not learn to feel joy and sadness, or how to think about things. Life is a continuing, connected dance.

When we are close to nature—at the seashore, in the woods, watching a sunset or playing with animals—we can feel the spirit of Gaia in our own deep joy. We feel it as her children, and the way we feel it is the only way we can imagine her feeling it.

So let us go back to the time, billions of years ago, when we can imagine Gaia feeling joyful and proud at how well things were going with oxygen. Somehow she knew when it reached just the right amount to keep herself and her children healthy. A little less oxygen in the air and they could not breathe, a little more and everything would catch fire! Ever since that time she has kept the balance of oxygen makers and oxygen users just as was needed in the dance of life.

 Eventually her tiny bacteria covered Earth. The seas, the rocks and the atmosphere teemed with them. All their molecules were of Earth, of Gaia's own body. In other words, part of her body had transformed itself into these living creatures. But so far there was not a single plant or animal, not even a cell with a nucleus in it.

8

PARTNERS IN A NEW DANCE

The ancient bacteria—the archea we've been talking about—were cells, but not the kind of cells that plants and animals are made of. Plants and animals would never have come to be if the early bacteria had simply gone on living as they were.

Bacteria are nowadays called prokaryotes. Pro means before, and karyon—pronounced CArry-on—means kernel or nucleus. So prokaryotes – said pro-CArry-oats—are cells before nuclei developed. Remember that the nucleus of a cell is the part with all the DNA in it. In a prokaryote, or bacterium, which has no nucleus, the DNA floats around loosely in the cell as a long string, often joined into a loop.

With this loose arrangement, the DNA and proteins and other chemicals in the prokaryotes managed to do a lot of wonderful things. There are still endlessly different kinds of bacteria on Earth today, and so many of each kind that a single spoonful of natural soil swarms with billions of bacteria. Some are hardy creatures, able to live high up in the atmosphere, deep down in the oceans, inside boiling hot springs and freezing cold ice.

No other living creatures could have evolved on Earth without bacteria as their ancestors. Bacteria can turn pure stone and water into food for themselves and for other living things. They are forever at work making rich soil for plants to grow in, living very helpfully inside animals and turning dead plants and animals back into more rich soil by decaying them.

Rot and decay are just bacterial ways of recycling. What a wonderful thing for us that they do it so that no wastes pile up in nature. We still have a lot to learn from them!

Bacteria can afford to keep small streamlined bodies, for when they need new DNA instructions for some new task, they can get it from other bacteria by dissolving their cell membranes to exchange bits of DNA and then repair the membranes. Humans, who recently discovered this, call it 'genetic engineering' and take credit for it as a human discovery! Because of their constant DNA trading, bacteria are, in a way, like a single huge organism or organ. We could think of them as Gaia's living skin.

Viruses may have been the archebacs's way of living through hard times. What if they could store just their DNA genes in packets resistant to extreme heat or cold or dryness? When times got better, the tiny packets could be taken in by surviving bacterial cells whose proteins could open them up and add the stored DNA to their own. Perhaps this is how the first viruses came to be. Maybe viruses cause trouble when their DNA packets are opened by creatures they were not intended for.

Bacteria help keep all the gases in our atmosphere balanced in just the right amounts. They also balance the chemicals in the seas and soil. They are the caretakers of all other living things, Gaia's most important workers.

There is probably no better example of cooperation in the dance of life than the cooperation of bacteria all over our planet—the tiniest creatures doing the greatest jobs in managing things. It has taken us a very long time to realize just how cooperative and helpful bacteria are. After all, they are much too tiny to see, so they do their work invisibly—unless we study them with electron microscopes, which are still quite a new invention.

Compared with all the wonderful things they do, it doesn't seem hard to forgive them if once in a while they don't get along with cells in our bodies and our cells fight with them and that fight makes us sick. Even this has been an interesting challenge for us, and we have learned to use other bacteria to cure many sicknesses. On the whole, bacteria do far more to keep us healthy than to make us sick.

The more we study them, the more amazing they are to us. We have already talked about the surprising discovery that they live not only on our skins and in our guts, but that they are built right into our own cells—that tiny mitochondria have their own DNA, like independent little creatures, and make our energy for us. The way this came about is a fascinating and ancient story we are just now learning. It seems to go something like this:

Back in the ancient seas and on land and in the air, all different kinds of bacteria were trying out new ways of making their energy and of getting around to find food. We already know about the oxygen makers and the oxygen users, as well as the earliest kind from whom both are descended and which largely went underground to escape oxygen.

Let us call these original archebacs, which fermented their food for a living, bubblers as we usually see bubbles of their waste gases wherever they are at work in muddy swamps or in beer and bread, where we have harnessed them to help make food for us! And let us call the oxygen makers, recalling their colors, bluegreens, ancestors of chloroplasts. Then we can call the later-evolving oxygen users breathers, ancestors of mitochondria.

At some point, breathers, running out of supply molecules to break up with oxygen, seem to have invaded the larger more sluggish bubblers to use their molecules as food. The invaders were hi-tech breathers who had invented tails attached to them by motors. These tails twisted and lashed to move them around much faster than blobby bubblers that could only go where the waters floated them. The tails helped them drill their way into the big bubblers.

Perhaps some of the breathers bumped into the bubblers and could not drill into them, getting stuck onto their outsides instead. Wriggling around, they might have moved the whole bubbler cell along. With such tails, the big cell could moved around and find more food of its own. Perhaps it ended up feeding the breathers in turn for driving them.

Somewhere in such archea adventures, bluegreens also invaded these bubblers, or perhaps just went along for the ride into waters where there was enough light for them to make a living. The oxygen they made would also have been of use to the breathers.

As the bluegreens and breathers divided to multiply within the big bubblers, they became giant colonies, sometimes moving along with their many little tails attached like oars. Somehow, these three kinds of archebacs, which had begun by exploiting each other, ended up as partners in a cooperative venture! That may have been the most important step ever in Gaia's evolving dance.

 Sooner or later all the tiny partners must have found it hard to cooperate smoothly without some kind of organization of their work. Maybe the records and plans in the loose DNA were getting too scrambled when the individual cells divided, or when the bacteria traded DNA information with each other.

Whatever happened, some of these complex colonies finally got themselves organized and created the nuclear library of DNA we already know about from donations by the cooperative's members. Each of the bacteria donated DNA and all of it together was enclosed in a protective sack. That is how the nucleus evolved for storing, retrieving and copying information for running the huge new cell.

Some of the partners, such as the bluegreens and breathers, kept enough of their own DNA to continue evolving to do their own special work as chloroplasts and mitochondria. They no longer had enough DNA to be able to live independently outside the cooperatives, so they were committed to remain forever inside the new cells. Because cells with nuclei are no longer prokaryotes, we call them eukaryotes, which is said you-CArry-oats and means 'with nuclei'.

A shorter name for eukaryotes is protists. Protists are on average a thousand times bigger than bacteria, sometimes much bigger than that! From the time they came into being there were both archebacs that continued living by themselves or in colonies without walls—and the huge protist cooperatives. Archebacs and protists are both single-cell creatures, as we know. Yet, we could say, for fun, that protists are multi-creatured cells since they are made up of many archebacs! Later, we will see that they form cooperatives called multi-celled creatures, but that is getting ahead of our story.

Long before they formed protists, the archebacs had simpler ways of dividing. Sometimes a small bud broke off the parent cell, taking along some of the DNA and other cell parts to start a new life on its own. Sometimes the cells split into many small parts, just like each other. And sometimes a single cell split into two equal parts. But no matter how they did it, all the baby cells came from a single parent and were, except for the occasional DNA copying mistakes, exactly like that parent.

You may wonder, if they copied themselves so exactly, how could they have evolved into such different kinds as bubblers, bluegreens and breathers? The answer is, because they could trade DNA with each other freely. All they had to do was snuggle up to each other, rubbing a hole in their touching cell membranes and trading bits of DNA with each other.

The cell membranes were quickly repaired, but the two were now different from what they were before their union. This way of making new creatures from different DNA sources is technically called sex. And this kind of sex goes on freely among all bacteria to this day. It has nothing to do with reproduction, so we could call it 'safe sex.'

The way they divided, or reproduced themselves, is called fission, and this was kept up by the nucleated protists, but it meant they had to make a copy of the nucleus before dividing so that each offspring cell would have a whole nucleus just like the one from which it was copied, as we have learned. What was no longer possible was sex. They could no longer trade around their DNA as they liked.

Some protists found a way around this loss of sex, of making new cells that were not just like the originals.

If they hadn't, their evolution into other creatures might have been slowed up. The new kind of reproduction probably came about through a series of lucky accidents. However it happened, we call it sexual reproduction because it combines sex—the merging of DNA from different individuals—and the division called reproduction.

To see how it works, think back to the DNA zippers unzipping themselves, but stop the dance before the new partner-teeth are chosen by the half zippers. Imagine now that a cell divides right then, so that each zipper sends half of itself into one new cell and half into the other.

Such cells, of course, were not complete. They couldn't do anything until their zippers were made whole. But they found a way of doing that without choosing one new tooth-partner at a time. They looked around for other half-zipper cells made from the same kind of parent bacteria and found they could match up zipper halves by joining together as one single cell. Instead of each tooth finding a new partner, one half-zipper could team up with another!

We already know that DNA dancers are organized into genes that are codes for proteins and for other things we still don't understand but know are needed for forming and running cells. Half-zippers of DNA can only match up with each other if the genes for each protein are at the same place in the line. That is why the half-zipper cells must find partners from the same kind of parent—the kind that has the genes lined up the same way.

Gaia's dance became very lively with the new protists, each about a thousand times as big on average as the archebacs from which they had been formed. Of course the archebacs remaining independent continued to thrive alongside them, continuing to do their vital work.

If you have ever looked at a drop of pond water under a microscope, you will have an idea of what some protists look like. Paramecia, for example, are easily found in puddles and ponds, looking like tiny slippers rowed along by hundreds of wavy oars. Big blobby amoebae change their shapes before your eyes, moving about by pushing out what look like temporary arms and legs.

Some protists with loads of chloroplasts—the bluegreen oxygen makers –became algae. Lots of algae stuck together can be seen as greenish patches on pond water or stuck together on rocks at the seashore. Green algae make lots and lots of oxygen. Some of them joined together in long strings or flat sheets we call seaweed, as if they were plants. But plants are always multi-cell creatures and algae are single cells even if they live in colonies.

 Other protists, living by themselves, tried out fancy shapes for their cell walls, as if they were trying to see who could make the most beautiful ones. The most fantastic walls of all were made by radiolarians that still build amazing shapes we can see under microscopes—shapes like king's crowns and very fancy blown-glass Christmas tree ornaments.

Other specialized protists called diatoms give us a clue to how Gaia keeps exactly the right balance of salt in the sea. Rivers flowing into the sea carry salts and minerals that the water dissolves out of the rocks it flows over. Gaia needs these salts and minerals in the sea, but like the oxygen in the air there must not be too much of them or they would choke off living creatures.

One such mineral is silica. Hundreds of millions of tons of it are washed into the seas every year. Silica is exactly what diatoms and radiolarians use to build their shells. There are so many gazillions of these protists in the seas that they use up much of it. When they die, they sink to the bottom, leaving their silica shells to settle into more rock. Three-hundred million tons of silica rock every year!

And so, the rivers keep bringing silica to the seas and the radiolarians and diatoms wear it brilliantly while they live and then turn it into harmless rock. There are always just enough of them to keep the right amount of silica dissolved in the sea for other creatures to use. As we learn about such things, we learn more and more about Gaia's cooperative dance of life—about how she looks after all her creatures to keep them in balance with each other, and to keep her whole planet self healthy.

Rock forms from diatoms and other sediments as they are pressed together over long periods of time at the bottom of the seas. This rock may be pushed out of the seas eventually as new land, or it may be pushed back down through Earth's crust at the edges of the great tectonic plates that make Earth's crust movable, like the plates of an armadillo's armor. When it is pushed back down under the edge of another plate, it is melted back into magma so it can be cycled again into lava coming up through volcanoes or oozing out between plate edges as they spread apart deep beneath the oceans.

We see then that even Earth's crust is active in circulating supplies and rearranging itself. Life is, in fact, rock rearranging itself into living creatures and then back into rock, into new geological features and then into new living creatures!

From our tiny one-celled ancestors, the eukaryotes or protists, all the larger fungi, plants and animals of Earth evolved. Many of them hooked together as strings or blobs and then into more complex colonies, learning how to stay together and do different jobs. Eventually they also evolved the ability to reproduce those colonies, and that is how they formed multi-celled creatures—the fungi, plants and animals.

But before we go on to see how larger creatures developed, let's think for a moment about how much the cells in our bodies are still like those first eukaryote cells in the seas, hundreds of millions of years ago. Our cells still have the same kind of nuclei in them, with the same kind of DNA, though the DNA plans have gotten much more elaborate.

Every cell has a wall around it, like the peel of an orange, and water within still very much like seawater, in which our proteins swim about doing their work to keep us alive. This seawater, along with most of our proteins, has been passed along from parents to their offspring ever since the early Earth times we have been talking about.

When creatures left the seas to live on land, they carried this supply of life-giving seawater along inside their cells, as we still do today. Inside this liquid, as you will remember, the mitochondria made of proteins, whose ancestors were archaia, make our energy, just as they have been making energy for all plants and animals since they first appeared on Earth.

In this way we are still connected to our earliest ancestors, and are very much a part of Gaia's dance—the creative dance of endless new steps making endlessly new kinds of creatures, though the first steps are never forgotten. How wonderful it is to know that every living being, from diatoms to the tallest pines, from microbes to butterflies and buffaloes, are all our relatives, all dancing with us in Gaia's great dance.

9

THE DANCE OF EVOLUTION

When we say that our own cells, our whole bodies, are descendants of the first cells on Earth, we are of course talking about evolution. Evolution, as we are seeing, is the development of complex creatures from earlier, simpler kinds. In just the same way, you will remember, dancers use the word evolution for the development of new dance patterns from simpler movements and steps.

It is still a great puzzle for scientists to figure out just how the changes happened between the archebacs and ourselves, or any other being alive today. These changes happened over billions of years and the long chains of evolution from our ancestors are hard to track down.

Fortunately, many of them left us clues. Shells and bones that gradually turned into stone after they died, and body prints left in soft mud that hardened into rock, are called fossils. Fossils can tell us a lot about plants and animals that lived long ago, and we can compare them with those that live now. There are even fossil bacteria!

Scientists have ways to tell just how old fossils are and we know that the oldest fossils of all are fossils of the first living cells. When fossils are put in the order of how long ago they lived, we can easily see that creatures got more complex as time went on. And often we can discover who were whose descendants.

One of the important things fossils tell us are which creatures did not change very much over time. For instance, some very ancient cells were very much like some bacteria still living today, or like our own mitochondria, as we have seen.

Today's squids and sharks are very like their ancestors, who swam the seas long before true fishes came to be. In a way, that makes them living fossils that can be compared with the kinds of creatures that kept on changing, or evolving over many generations.

Evolution, like any dance, has its own rhythms. Some kinds, or species, of creatures, such as the squids and sharks, or ants and cockroaches and opossums, seem to have come almost to a standstill. They've been passing on the same body design from parents to young for millions of years. Other species have made changes so quickly—which means in so few generations—that they seem almost to leap from being one kind of creature to being quite a different kind. In a way, the kind that stay the same are like bicycles in a world of jet planes. Bicycles still work very well as they are, but they have also been steps along the road to inventing jets.

Fossils alone cannot actually prove that one species turned into another. Of all the creatures that have lived on Earth, only some turned into fossils or left fossil prints. And of course we cannot go digging up the whole Earth looking for them, so those we find are far fewer than those there are. This makes it very hard to line up just that string of fossils which show all the changes, say from a cow-like ancient animal to a modern whale.

But if we look at fossils of animals and plants that lived long ago, we see interesting similarities with—and differences from—those alive today. Some are so much the same that we can be sure modern sharks descended directly from ancient ones. But Gaia tried out many designs that did not survive to modern times. Sometimes they didn't survive because they turned into new designs; other times their family line simply ended because they couldn't adjust to changes in their world and died out.

You know that Earth was once full of dinosaurs. The fossil record reveals them in all shapes and sizes, up to a certain time around sixty million years ago when they disappeared suddenly. We are still not sure exactly why they died out, but there is evidence of a giant meteor or planetoid striking Earth that could have changed the climate hugely over a short period of time. Whatever the catastrophe was, it must have changed conditions in which dinosaurs had lived so much that the dinosaurs' homes were destroyed and/or they could not find food or even enough oxygenated air to live.

Perhaps great earthquakes drained the water from their swamps, killing the things they lived off. Perhaps some great explosion out in space shocked Earth and changed its temperature just enough so their huge bodies did not work any longer. In any case, after the age of dinosaurs, only small reptiles and mammals show up in fossil records.

Just as many of Gaia's creatures were killed off earlier by dangerous oxygen and other later disasters, most of her dinosaurs were killed by some accident she suffered. Yet, once again, she managed to recover. Sometimes her disasters proved to be opportunities for new things to happen!

When we look at dinosaur fossils, we can see that today's reptiles, such as lizards and alligators, must have descended from the ones that survived. Yet, even before the great catastrophe, we find dinosaur fossils that were on the way to becoming birds.

Archeopteryx—which means ancient-wings in Greek—was a kind of dinosaur with horny beaks and strong wings with which they could fly through the air. Their skeletons look very much like those of today's birds. In their evolution, their reptile scales became feathers, their front legs became wings, their long snouts turned into beaks. Even today, birds lay eggs, just as their reptile ancestors did and just as modern reptiles do.

Fossils give us a chance to see bits and pieces of evolution, and to try to arrange them in order so that we can guess at the missing pieces. Luckily, Gaia gives us other clues besides fossils to show how she went about evolving her creatures.

When we look at the bones of all the animals living today, and at their eyes and teeth, their brains and hearts and other organs, we can see how they are related to each other. We can see what kinds of designs had to come before other designs. Just as people had to invent carts pulled by horses before they could think up cars with engines, Gaia had to try out simple eyes and brains before complicated ones that worked better could evolve.

We can see that human brains could only evolve from simpler mammal brains, and mammal brains could only evolve from simpler reptile brains, and reptile brains from even earlier brains so simple they were hardly brains at all.

If you could look inside your own head, you would see evolution at work. The deepest part of your brain, and everyone else's, looks very much like an old-model reptile brain. On top of it, and around it, there is another part that, together with the deep brain, looks much like the brains of mammals such as horses and lions. On top of all that, wrapped around it like the thinking cap it is, you would find the part of the brain special to people. It is called the cortex and makes it possible for us to talk, to become artists or scientists, to invent things and to learn and think about our relationship to all other creatures, to our whole planet and universe.

Our whole bodies show us even more than just our brains about how evolution happens. A baby growing inside its mother, as we all did, learns the whole beautiful dance of evolution!

Every one of us began as a single cell. A cell with a nucleus of DNA, lots of tiny mitochondria and other cell parts floating around in seawater with a protecting wall around it. Half the cell's DNA came from our father, the other half from our mother.

That cell divided into two, the two into four, then eight, then sixteen, thirty-two, sixty-four and so on until there was a ball-shaped creature looking very much like the simplest multi-celled creatures in the sea. And, indeed, it lives in a sea of its own—a special bag of liquid like seawater deep inside its mother.

If you watched a movie of its development, you would soon see the ball creature change its shape magically as its cells keep dividing again and again. One side of the ball dents in to from a groove, then a lumpy head appears at one end and a backbone begins to form. Soon it looks like a tiny tadpole with eyes in its big head and a long tail that starts twitching. A little later we all looked so much like the developing babies of fish and turtle and chickens and pigs it would be hard to tell which we were going to turn into!

There is of course no air to breathe, and the liquid passes in and out of our embryo bodies through little gill slits such as sea creatures have. Even when we develop the four tiny buds that begin our arms and legs, we still look like other kinds of baby animals developing and growing.

Slowly our bodies go on forming as we roll about comfortably in our warm sea. Our tails shrink to nothing, our brains grow bigger, our arms and legs and faces begin to look human. Finally, after nine months, we come out of our sea and begin to breathe the air.

It is as if hundreds of millions of years of evolution all happen in these nine months. As if Gaia reminds us just who we are and where we came from so we will never forget our part in the dance. In each of us, she seems to remember it from the beginning.

For a long time people thought all the different creatures of Earth had been created at the same time, just as they are now. They saw the creatures as they are and did not know they could have been any different. They didn't even know how old Earth is, so they didn't know how much time there has been for evolution to happen. They hadn't dug around for fossils and didn't know anything about DNA or proteins.

One of the first people to understand and explain evolution was a man named Charles Darwin, who lived in the 1800s. His explanation was very good for his time, but we have improved it a lot with all the things we have learned since then.

Darwin could see that changes happened between one generation and the next when people breed animals, such as dogs or pigeons. If people want whiter pigeons, or ones with longer beaks, they can select only the whitest or longest beaked ones from each generation to be the parents of the next. After enough generations, all the pigeons will be white or have long beaks, by the breeder's continuing selection.

Animals change in nature, too, as Darwin could see. Something seems to be selecting them so that they gradually change into different species. But there are no breeders to do it, so nature must be doing it herself. He called this 'natural selection' and figured out how it could work.

Every animal lives in some environment, where it hunts for food, finds a mate, has babies and protects them from other hunters. Every animal has babies that are not all exactly alike. Their differences are variations of their parents' body designs and some natural variations that happen by accidents in copying DNA, as we saw.

Some of the variations help the babies more than others at growing up and living in their environments. Longer beaks, if they were birds, would help them dig deeper for worms; thicker coats, if they were mammals, would help them survive cold winters; stronger wings, if they were insects, would help them get away from birds.

Most animals make so many babies that all of them do not survive. But many babies also means many variations from which the environment can 'select'. Those that had varied by unlucky accidents never grew up to pass on their variations to more babies. The lucky ones did survive, and so their variations were passed on to babies of their own.

If animals wandered out of their own environments and still survived, the new environment would 'select' different designs among their babies than the old environment would have. If it was warmer, for instance, thinner coats would be fitter than thicker coats. What fits one environment may not fit another. New environments, selecting for different variations, made it possible for one species of animal—or plant, for that matter—to branch into two.

Descendants of the same original parents could settle in two different environments and so become ever more different from each other with each new generation. Eventually, their genes would no longer line up with each other if they tried to make babies together. And that would mean they were two separate species. Making separate species is a way of making new designs without getting them all mixed up.

In this way, plant and animal designs had chances of improving further with each new generation in what came to be called the "survival of the fittest." This really should mean "those who fit best into their environment," though most people took it to mean "the strongest or best" in a competition because Darwin saw it that way—evolution through competition for survival.

Other scientists studying evolution, such as the Russian biologist Pyotr Kropotkin, saw a great deal of cooperation in nature. This idea – that cooperation as well as competition could help species survive and shape the changes we call evolution – should not surprise us. We have already seen a great example of this in the huge evolutionary leap from competitive archebacs to their protist cooperatives—the kind of cells we are made of.

What those tiny archebac cells discovered as they formed giant cooperatives evolving into nucleated protists became the biggest secret in evolution:

It is cheaper to feed your enemies than to kill them!

That means, it takes less energy, so it is more efficient to make friends of enemies. And, presto!, when you do that, you have no more enemies, just friends who can invent more ways to cooperate with no fighting expenses.

There was fierce completion among different kinds of bacteria in their youthful phase, but this discovery about cooperation is a clear sign of their coming to maturity, just as it is always a sign of greater maturity in children when they cooperate rather than fight.

In Darwin's day, people didn't much like being told they were descended from apes and were still their cousins. But the idea of nature selecting competitors appealed to them. They saw that as a test of nature in which all the individuals were competing to survive and only the best ones won. Seeing that wild animals eat each other they also thought animals were at war with each other in a bloody struggle for survival. This made them feel better about the things they were doing themselves.

Men competed with each other to make the best machines, and to get rich and powerful. They fought bloody wars and took over peoples' lands in other parts of the world. If those people couldn't protect themselves, they reasoned, that simply meant they were not fit. Being fit lost its meaning of fitting into an environment and came only to mean being fit as in being stronger or otherwise more powerful.

In Darwin's Europe and in America, where more and more Europeans were settling, scientists did not see cooperation in nature. Wherever they did see order and harmony, they thought it was brought about by 'the law of the jungle,' in which strong creatures ruled over weaker ones by natural right. People talked a lot about the natural rights of the fittest in a world of competition where everyone was out for himself.

Remember that they were also looking at creatures as living machines, changed by mechanical accidents and better or worse because of them. They did not pay much attention to Darwin's idea that no species was better than any other, or that many different kinds of creatures depended on each other. All they could see was a great 'struggle for survival,' as they called it. It wasn't a very nice picture of the world, and luckily it wasn't very true, either.

We can think up many ways of saying which creatures are fitter than others. We could say the fittest are those who make most of themselves, such as beetles, which come in a quarter of a million different species with a huge number of individuals in each one. Or we might say the fittest are those that fit changing environments over millions of years without having to change their designs, such as ants and squids and cockroaches. But these ideas all lead to arguments. The best way to look at evolution is to see how all species fit together in the dance of life.

- 10 -

The dance of co-evolution

Since the time of Darwin, more than a hundred years ago, we have learned a lot about just what an ecosystem really is. It is not so much a place into which creatures must fit themselves as it is a dance of living things interweaving themselves in a particular piece of Earth.

Swarms of bacteria busily keep the air, water and soil in balance; tiny insects and worms recycle things, each in their own way; fungi and plants interweave, from those too small to see to the tallest trees or giant sea grasses. Birds, fishes, reptiles and mammals all play their parts in an ecosystem making homes and food for each other.

A creature's 'fitness' is truly a matter of how well it fits into the dance of other creatures, which is the dance of their ecosystem. Way back at the beginning of this book we talked about how "each of us depends on the health of these ecosystems as much as each of the cells in our bodies depends on the rest of our body for its life." All creatures together evolve the dance of their ecosystems, ever changing that dance just to keep in balance, sometimes making up new steps—new ways of doing things, new creature designs.

No species can evolve all by itself, or just by competing with others. Evolution is always cooperative evolution, or co-evolution, for short. What people call 'environments' are actually ecosystems of countless creatures, large and small, rocks and rivers, soils and air in which everything has a role in creating everything else.

Even the predator-prey relationships we see so often on TV are cooperative if you think about it. Say you see lions hunting antelopes. The lions take only the weakest ones and never more than they need to eat and feed their young. Yes, the prey feeds the predator, but the lion also keeps the antelope species healthy by leaving the ones who run fast enough to escape lions to make more antelopes. You could say that lions are the antelopes' physical trainers.

If nature still feels unfair to you, imagine trying to design a better kind of nature. You have a wonderful planet to begin with, but you have to recycle what it offers to keep your system evolving, to keep it going. Life must recycle life. Even we humans have to eat other living creatures, whether plants or animals. That does not mean we can mistreat them in growing them for food, as our industrialized societies are now doing to both plants and animals on their factory farms.

Indigenous people, who did not industrialize, depended more directly on their ecosystems and understood other creatures as relatives and friends. One Native American story tells about a Mouse longing to fly like an Eagle. One day Eagle captures and eats Mouse. Mouse then becomes part of Eagle's body and is happy because it now sees through the eyes of Eagle flying high over everything! To tell such stories, Native people clearly believed in the Oneness of all nature and the spirit in things that lives on through death. They understood well that without death there can be no recycling.

Earth's whole surface of land, seas and sky is filled with living things. Because that surface is ball-round, living creatures spreading over it met up with each other. Even long before any plants or animals evolved, the archebacs covered Earth and worked together in creating the oxygen-rich air, the food-rich sea and the nutrient-rich soil.

Earlier we said life could be seen as "rock rearranging itself." The bacteria covering Earth are made of earth, or soil—gathering the minerals of rock and the water of seas into their mostly protein selves, as we saw. If we could follow the life stories of the same atoms or even molecules through different Earth ages, they might be part of the rocky crust at some times and part of living creatures at others.

We also saw earlier that the dead bodies of living things form sediments in the seas that are pressed back into rock. This rock is eventually molten and recycled through volcanoes before it is transformed again into living creatures. Despite the slow speed of rock's recycling, there is hardly any rock on the surface of Earth that has not been made, at least partly, of living creatures.

Looking at Earth as a whole this way, we see the movement of the great tectonic plates circulating rock throughout Gaia's body as she dances—as molten magma flowing slowly beneath the surface, then as the cooled rock of her skin. The rock is transformed into microbes, fungi, plants and animals. As they die, their bodies are pressed back into soils and seafloors. Eventually they are pressed so deep into the tectonic plates that the sliding and heat turns them back into magma.

Rock is not all that gets recycled in the living Earth's body. Seawater is also recycled through living bodies, though more slowly than air. Yet seawater is recycled faster than rock. And every molecule of air you breathe has recently been through another living creature's body! Was it your cat? The kids down the street? The grass and trees nearby, or those birds? The microbes on your skin and clothing? The breeze that came from the South? The steam pouring from your Mom's kitchen? It could be all of those, but surely is much more. Who or what will next be breathing the air you are breathing out now?

This is what it means to be in co-creation with all living things. You are totally connected into your world. The world creates you as you create the world. More on this later!

On planets such as Venus and Mars, there is no ecosystem in which living things can live—because there are no living things to create ecosystems together and for each other. There are no circulation systems of rock, water and air, and so these planets cannot come to life. Also, as we said earlier, one is too hot, the other too cold. Only planets with moving, changing parts and favorable temperatures can be living, evolving planets.

 Both Venus and Mars have unchanging atmospheres made mostly of carbon dioxide. It's easy to remember what carbon dioxide is if we look at the atoms its molecules are made of. In each one, a single carbon atom dances with two oxygen atoms, di meaning two. The oxygen makers on Earth use the energy of sunlight to split off the carbon atom and use it to build their bodies. The twin oxygen atoms are released as oxygen gas, which is why we call them oxygen makers. They fill the air with oxygen and, after they die, their carbon atoms end up buried as part of them in the ground or sea bottom

On the other hand, the oxygen users keep putting carbon dioxide back together and releasing it back into the air. All living things need carbon to build their molecules, and there is always a rich supply of it buried in the ground as well as floating in the water and air.

Air is much the same all over our planet because it moves around quickly and so keeps getting stirred up into an even mixture. Seas flow all around Earth as well, but not as fast as air. The balance of chemicals in the sea is kept by tiny creatures within the sea, such as the diatoms we learned about. The surface of the seas and shallow waters near the shores get more light and heat energy from the Sun, so they were good places for life to evolve when Gaia was young.

Bacteria also make and use other gases in our atmosphere. And here is something very interesting: If they and other living creatures ever stopped, the gases in our atmosphere would burn each other up, leaving mostly carbon dioxide as on Mars and Venus! The only reason our atmosphere stays as it is, is because it is constantly renewed by living things, and kept in balance by them.

How amazing that the whole system stays in the perfect balance for life, without any species in charge, yet all of them playing their roles.

Let's go back now to the time when creatures were building themselves into different kinds of cells. Remember that the archebacs went through a very long phase of youthful creativity and competition before they began cooperating to form the nucleated cells called protists. Just so, the new giant protist cooperatives—just because they were new—had to go through their own phase of youthful creativity and competition. During that phase, they evolved into many, many shapes and kinds of protists making their living in countless clever ways.

Eventually, they, too, discovered the advantages of cooperation and began forming multi-celled creatures. In other words, they discovered it was cheaper to feed your enemies than to kill then and grew up into cooperative maturity.

These new multi-celled creatures, which were actually protist cooperatives, now took their turn at being a youthful new kind of living creature in Gaia's dance. Eventually, they matured into the tightly interwoven species of cooperative ecosystems. That is co-evolution!

Journey of a Silica Atom

I am an atom of silica
born from the belly of a super nova star
flung far into space in its last burst of glory
drawn into the great wheel of its dust cloud
congealed into a planet with a hot molten core.
For eons I roll in slow waves of magma
deep below the planet's thickening crust
at last pushing upward to the mouth of a great volcano
spewed forth splendidly
a spray of fire against the black night sky.
I come to rest in glossy black basalt
waiting patiently until the rains
dislodge me from this barren unmoving rock
washing me suddenly into a tumbling rivulet
down to a river and on to the sea.
Oh! the glory of it as I am snatched up and
bound into the crystal shell of a radiolarian
wondrous designs of the sea's tiny creatures
delicate as blown glass ornaments
splendid as the crowns of kings.
But little good my short-lived vanity as I sink
to the seafloor and am swallowed up in a trilobite's gut;
then yet again swallowed by an imperious nautilus
huffing and puffing its jetway through the dark waters
as it builds me into its striped hull.
What great upheaval now is this
as the Earth's very belly rumbles and my nautilus,
to whom I have grown so attached, as we say
is hurtled onto dry ground
as the waters recede?
Here my star dust is ground to Earth dust
as the crustal agony thrusts plate against great crustal plate

and I blow—still one atom of silica—across new mountains
in red sand storms till coming to rest again
where shallow inland seas slowly give rise to swamps.
Here I become flesh-eating plant and dragonfly wing;
whatever absorbs me paying the price of dissolving again
that other things may form. I live on now
in great scaly trees one after another,
until I am buried into Earth
beneath the heavy stomp of tail-dragging dinosaurs.
I am coal, fellow to legions of carbon atoms
with their own tales to tell through the long night of rest
in the quiet beneath the surface of Earth.
Who knows how often the seas come and go above us
the deserts dry and the rains return?
At last the bowels of the Earth shake once more
and I suddenly see the light of day exciting my lust
for new travels. Gone are the great swamps and stompings—
or are they? for here come thundering buffalo herds
to graze the land far and wide.
In blades of prairie grass
I soon make their intimate acquaintance
traveling their long guts only to grow into new grass
with each renewed cycle of birth and death.
The pattern is broken when flood rains relieve the bondage
and I continue my journey in swirling waters
until a filament of fungus catches me
along some sandy bank
and draws me into itself.
The fungus lives among the roots of plants
trading nourishment—and one day I am traded
Sucked up along roots into stem and then leaf
where I glisten in sun and rain while the plant
makes its food and lives its life.
One day a deer comes nibbling by the bank and
lo I am there in its dark warm insides
ever moving through its bloodstream and cells

until the deer is brought down by a wolf.
I am left behind after wolf and cubs feast
for vultures and worms and flies
and legions of tinier microbes—the great recyclers
not knowing which of them
will send me on my way again.
As it happens I travel on in the shell of a small beetle
who meets her end in the mouth of a frog
who no sooner having swallowed me
is himself recycled through a great white heron
who excretes my bit of beetle shell
unceremoniously and still undigested back into the river
where waters dissolve my chip of beetle wing
releasing me to tumble freely once more.
Now on the glistening surface
a gust of wind lifts me high into the air
higher and higher into a thick grey cloud
and then still higher into white wispy strands
that blow to colder climes.
Oh! newest of adventures high in the sky
over the low spring arctic sun
crystallizing into a snowflake
falling back to Earth's white cover
where I wait for the summer melt.
Tumbling again through bright clear streams
flanked by fields of flowers
I wash once more to the sea.
Gone are the trilobites, the lifeforms once I knew
but oh! what marvelous times befall me now
as I cycle through plankton and seagrass and fishes
tubeworms and lobsters in seas chill and tropic
thrilling to the great diversity
ever renewing my role in
the great dance of life.
Are they eons passing now or only moments?
as I lie amidst the oceans' sediment

pressed ever downward
as layers of sand and mud settle over me
ground along in the spreading seafloor until
it meets the edge of another crustal plate.
Pushed downward ever deeper
the old familiar heat of Earth's core warms me
back into the molten magma where this journey began
back among my fellows
whose tales of adventure rival my own.
We know the Earth's body
in all its magnificent twists and turns
We know its life intimacies:
the thrill and speed of cataracts
the measured step of thundercloud
the leisure of mountain and meadow,
the peaceful fall of the snows.
We know the heat of the desert
and its cold beneath the moon
we know the moor and mountain
for we have been microbes, fungus and plants
we have soared with the beetles and birds
we have been the fishes in the depths of the sea
and the creatures who fish them in turn
There is no part of Earth's body
in which we have not shared
the ever improvisational dance of life
How many silica atoms are dancing in you?

____

- 10 -

IMPROVISATION IN THE DANCE

Co-evolution was not designed in advance but happened as creatures tried out all these ways of life in Gaia's dance. We call that kind of dance improvisational or 'improv' for short—a dance that the dancer or dancers make up as they go. They do not know themselves what will happen next as they improvise!

Let's review their evolutionary leaps. First the archebacs begin their lives as molecular cooperatives made of proteins, fats, sugars and acids (the stored information molecules of RNA/DNA). Secondly, protists come to life as archebac cooperatives. Thirdly, multi-celled creatures come to life as cooperatives of different kinds of protists. At each stage larger cooperatives were formed in the dance.

What we see in this sequence is that every big leap in evolution has been about the cooperation that happens when a new kind of creature gets through its youth to grow up into its maturity through discovering the advantages of cooperation. During its youth it competes and uses up resources as fast as possible in a Darwinian way while reproducing madly. Then it discovers that cooperation has the wonderful advantage that it is far less exhausting than endless competition because it takes less energy. And it offers whole new possibilities for creating larger and more complex life forms.

These three greatest steps in Gaia's improv dance of life took more than three billion years, which is three-quarters of Earth's life up to the present! Evolution seems to have been slow at the beginning and has been speeding up ever since. Now it is going so fast we have a hard time keeping up with our own changes in a single lifetime!

Let's go back to see how the new multi-celled creatures tried out different creature designs. One of the things they carried with them was the discovery of sexual reproduction—the combining of original sex with reproduction. Remember how they stored all the information for making themselves into certain cells that split into half-zipper cells? When these were released by the protists, they could find matching cells of the same kind to form new protists.

Some species tried out having more than two sexes—yes, that is biologically possible. For example, the paramecia we spoke of finding in pond water, when looking at life through a microscope, have eight different sexes, but two seemed to work out best as the dance of evolution went on—male and female.

In protists and early multi-celled creatures, male and female were often part of the same body. Some plants and animals still work that way today—earthworms, for instance, and many flowers. Even flowers that have both sexes cooperate with bees, by giving them nectar to make honey so the bees will carry the male pollen cells from one flower to another. They may not think about cooperation the way we do, but the knowledge of how to cooperate is there in both bees and flowers, as in the rest of nature.

As males and females became separate creatures in more and more species, they went on cooperating in the dance of life, making their babies by combining half-zipper cells. And so the ancient seas slowly filled with experiments in multi-celled creatures—crawling worms, floating jellyfish, microscopic animals that went on living in colonies as sponges and corals, clams and squids and all sorts of other designs.

Coral animals collected minerals in their bodies to make hard shells, which stayed in place as they died. From these, huge coral reefs were built up—the biggest things built by living creatures anywhere on Earth. These coral reefs became environments for ever more coral creatures and other creatures living in the reefs, which often look like great flowering gardens although they are made of animals.

Animals and plants sometimes got so mixed up together in early creatures that they are hard to fit into our systems of classifying them. Some of them became such specialists in using oxygen for energy that they gave up their sunlight-using chloroplasts and became animals. Maybe animals actually evolved from plants that lost their chloroplasts. Without them, they could not make food from soil, water and sunlight rooted solidly in one place. So they had to evolve ways of finding, chasing, catching and eating food. In other words, they had to evolve themselves into animals!

Gaia did lots of mixing and matching in her dance of evolution. Even today we find giant green clams using chloroplasts tucked into their skin to make some of their energy. And when we look at sea anemones, they look much more like flowers than the animals they are. Plants and animals can be much more closely related to each other than different kinds of bacteria!

Biologists talk about five life "kingdoms" on Earth: the prokaryote bacteria without nuclei are called Monera, and the one-cell prokaryote creatures are called Protoctists, which means "first builders" or just Protists for short. The third kingdom is the Fungi, such as molds and mushrooms, which are neither plants nor animals. Then, finally, there are the Plant and Animal kingdoms we know the best.

 Both plants and animals are many-celled, have mitochondria in their cells and mostly reproducing sexually. Plants, as you know, make most of their energy from sunlight using chloroplasts, while animals normally have no chloroplasts and get their energy from a variety of food they have to find and catch and eat.

All five kingdoms dance their lives together in ecosystems, depending on each other in complex ways. Bacteria, or monera, and plants making their energy from sunlight become food for other bacteria as well as for fungi and animals. The bodies of fungi, plants and animals, in turn, are taken apart molecule by molecule by bacteria when they die and so are turned into nutritious soil from which plants grow. Life and death are both important in Gaia's dance. Neither could happen without the other.

Death is never an end, but always a chance for a new beginning. This is Gaia's wisdom. She also uses challenges to keep life healthy. Each of her creatures has a will to live. Even though it must die sometime so that others may live, it tries to protect its life as long as it can.

From the time of the first complex ecosystem of single and many-celled creatures in the ancient seas, bigger creatures have been eating smaller creatures to live. When the bigger creatures die, the smaller ones get their turn to feed off them. The same creature might be good food for the one chasing it and bad news for the one it chases. Because of this, living things had to learn to protect themselves with shells or safe homes, or by swimming or running faster, or squirting clouds of ink around themselves so they couldn't be seen. They had to develop better eyes and teeth and claws and brains, or try out new colors and shapes to camouflage themselves. Camouflage is a way of looking so much like the things around you that you are not noticed by someone chasing you or by someone you want to catch.

There were other dangers, too—such as the danger of running out of food and having to move to new ecosystems. That meant learning new things to be able to live in the new places. When the first plants moved out of the sea and onto shores, they had to learn to make their bodies stronger so they could stand up without collapsing, and to keep themselves from drying up without seawater around them. When animals later followed the plants out of the seas they had to learn to breathe air, which meant they had to learn to make themselves lungs.

How could creatures learn such things? How could they change their designs in so many ways?

In the old mechanistic way of explaining evolution, they didn't learn these things at all. They just happened by genetic accident, and lucky accidents that improved life were automatically selected to stay in the genome and so were passed on to other generations. After all, a mechanism can only do what it is already built to do, and the only way it can change is by a mistake in the building, or by new combinations of genes from two parents. Which parents came together is considered as much a matter of accident as the mistakes in copying genes.

Darwin had said that if the small accidental change made the creature work better in its environment, then it would live to pass on the change to its young. These offspring would grow up stronger or better than the others, who would eventually weaken and die or be eaten or starve. The "fitter" surviving generations of offspring would then have to wait for new accidents in their own reproduction to keep on bringing further improvement in their designs.

This way of explaining things made it very hard to see how designs like eyes or wings could come about. It seems impossible that eyes could develop by one little accidental change after another if each change had to be useful by itself to be 'selected.'

An eye is an organ, and it has to be organized from a complex set of parts to work.

In the new way of explaining evolution we see that life organizes itself in intelligent and mostly cooperative ways. More and more scientists are recognizing that nature is impossible without being intelligent down to its simplest parts. Bacteria are very good at social networking to solve problems together. They can change themselves to digest new food they could not eat before, to protect themselves against ultraviolet rays as we saw, and do loads of other things we don't even know about yet. What is increasingly accepted, however, is that they do it intelligently.

We know that even chemicals far simpler than the simplest bacteria organize themselves to do new things. If the first protein molecules did form from the accidental blowing or floating about of smaller simpler sugar and acid molecules, further blowing and bumping about is not likely ever to have produced any kind of creature by accident. It takes enormous organization to create bacteria. And bacteria had to organize themselves to become protists as we saw, just as protists had to organize themselves into multi-celled creatures. Ecosystems are made of countless different kinds of creatures all working together with no one of them in charge!

Changing environments push creatures to organize and reorganize themselves, just as falling temperature pushes steam to reorganize its molecules into water, and water to reorganize its molecules into ice. Steam, water and ice all have the same molecules, but at each temperature they find the best way to rearrange the pattern of their dance into a better one for that temperature. Amazingly, though temperature changes gradually, the molecules reorganize suddenly at the boiling and freezing points. We can call those 'tipping points' where the pressure to change builds up gradually until it suddenly happens!

Living beings do similar things, and that is why evolution is not a smooth, gradual process of change. Compared with the long time bacteria were around, their organization into eukaryote cells—partnerships with nuclei—was quite sudden. Partly the environment pushed for changes, as when bacteria had to learn to turn oxygen from a bad thing into a good thing if they were to survive. Partly the early creatures experimented inside themselves to rearrange and evolve their patterns in this great improv dance.

Some patterns that don't work well at one time or in one place may work better in others. It seems that the protein and DNA genome learned to keep records of plans that were tried but failed. This gave it reserve plans for new emergencies. The genome of every living being contains far more plans than it ever uses. It looks as if they have been stored up all through evolution.

For example, scientists were very surprised to find genes from archebacs in the human genome! Such reserve plans may explain why some species have come up with new designs rather suddenly, in far fewer generations than it would take for accidental changes to pile up. And with better organization than accidents can explain. It is a long way from a few cells sensitive to light, to a working eye in a highly organized pattern. Chance accidents could never explain it.

Even Darwin recognized that was a problem with his theory. Now we can imagine that creatures tried different arrangements for seeing for a long time, failing but keeping records just as a person trying to invent something does. Suddenly, one day, an inventor may remember something she had tried long ago that might work now that she had made other kinds of progress on her invention.

Perhaps the first working eye suddenly came together from old plans, as sometimes happens to such careful and patient inventors. After that it could be improved more slowly by smaller changes. Actually, in evolution, it seems that eyes were invented a number of times by different species.

If creatures are to use reserve plans in new situations, they must keep themselves open for new developments. If they specialize too much, they will not be able to change. At the end of the great age of dinosaurs, the ones who had specialized in large bodies died. They could not go back to being as small as the ones that survived.

Many insects specialized in hard, thin body covers like suits of armor which could not grow bigger. That meant nothing inside could grow bigger either. We can tell they work well as they are, because they have survived a very long time, but it is hard for them to evolve any further. It seems that beetles will be beetles forever!

The best way Gaia found to go about evolution was to hold onto good designs but leave them open for some new improvisational changes. In the animal world, bones that grow bigger as the animal does turned out to be a good way to hold animal bodies together while leaving them room to develop in new ways. Four legs were good for walking. But leg design was left open enough in some animal species so that the same basic bone pattern could be changed into wings or flippers or arms to fit different environments and ways of life.

The story of evolution is more fascinating than any story people have ever made up to explain life on Earth. It is about creatures inventing themselves and each other in millions of different and daring designs. It is about the wonderful ways they have found to live together, feeding each other as creatures of a single living planet, with a single water system, a single air system and highly interwoven ecosystems. It is a story of adventure, competition, cooperation, improvisation, harmony and endless problems to be solved in new ways.

The old, mechanical way of looking at the world, with creatures simply evolving by accidents which fit or didn't fit them into their environments, was just too simple a view. And really not half as interesting as what we are discovering now about the intelligent self-organization of Gaia's improv dance. Remember that to improvise is to make it up as you go, using your intelligence to work out whatever problems come your way, and to correct imbalances so that all the dancers work together in harmony. Can we do this in our human world today?

Organization works best when it is cooperative and flexible. If it gets too rigid or too competitive, it does not work very well for long. We easily see this in the discontent people are now feeling about the old mechanical ways of organizing our schools, our work places and even our governments—as if they were supposed to work like well-oiled machines in which we were the parts! People now want to be treated like intelligent beings who can be improv dancers helping to reorganize such systems so they work better for us all.

Every living body larger than one cell, including your own, is an organization of intelligent cells that form organs, which in turn form organ systems within the overall systems of the whole body. Each body, along with the bodies of microbes, plants and other animals, is organized into ecosystems, such as coral reefs, deserts, forests and built human habitats. In each such ecosystem, creatures make each other's food supplies and homes. The most basic supplies of gases, water and minerals are circulated round and round in each ecosystem as though it were a kind of body itself. All these ecosystems together make up the greatest being of our planet—Gaia herself.

Gaia has gotten much more complex as creatures improvised and co-evolved, and so she needed ever more organization within her dance. Evolution is not just the development of large creatures from small ones, but this endless organization of the largest, smallest and in-between parts of the dance of co-evolution. Let's look more into this improvisational dance over time to see some of the steps in the part of the dance that evolved us people from early, simple creatures in the sea.

FROM POLYPS TO PEOPLE

Polyps were among the very first kinds of multi-celled animals in the ancient seas. Yet we still find them today, disguised in forms that make them look like plants. Sea anemones, looking like beautiful gardens of flowers, are polyp animals, and forests of coral are huge polyp colonies. Scientists call polyps cephalopods, which, in Greek, means 'headfoots'. That name describes them well.

The polyp animal is shaped like a tube with a flower-like circle of tentacles around the mouth at the head end. The foot end of the tube is stuck to a rock or another polyp body in its colony. And there it stays. It is a simple animal designed mainly for eating by catching its prey with its tentacles and stuffing the food into its mouth. Some of its cells are cleverly designed to sting and paralyze its prey.

Polyps started out reproducing by just budding off new ones, and they still do it that way. Colonies of polyps sometimes assign this job of reproduction to certain members while others feed them. In some species the new buds grow up stuck to the parent, but in others something quite different and more exciting happens.

The tiny bud breaks off, flips over so its tentacles are hanging down, and floats off into the sea. As it continues to eat and grow, it becomes a glassy umbrella with a fringed edge of trailing streamers—a jellyfish that is not a fish at all. The proper name of jellyfish is medusa, a name taken from the ancient myth of a woman with snakes for hair.

Medusae, which is plural for medusa, learned sexual reproduction. So they produce half-zipper egg cells and half-zipper sperm cells, just as other animals do. The egg and sperm cells join to make a still different creature, called a planula—a long, flattish blob with a fringe of rowing hairs around its edge. The planula swims free for a while, and then it settles onto a rock to turn into a polyp!

By evolving this life cycle, polyps got to spread themselves around and settle in new places with better food supplies. The grownup polyp stage is, however, one of those evolutionary specializations that reaches its end and can go no further. That is why polyps today still look like the ancient ones.

Perhaps the most amazing thing polyps have done can be seen in the Bluebottle Jellyfish, or Portuguese Man-o-War. This dreaded, poisonous creature is actually not a single animal at all, but rather a whole colony of polyps—four different kinds of them, all depending on each other to survive. Its float is a single bubble-shaped polyp; its tentacles are polyps that find and catch food and hand it over to other polyps that digest it. Still other polyps have the job of reproducing the Man-o-War. This reminds us of the ancient bacteria getting together in a division of labor when they formed the first nucleated cells.

Some of the free-swimming planulae seem to have decided it wasn't worth growing up and settling down into such a dull life. So they didn't. They began reproducing themselves as free swimming animals that never again settled down on rocks. They were improvising a whole new way of life!

It was as if Gaia got herself out of a blind alley of specialization by trying this new lifestyle with the young polyps while they were still free swimmers. Later we will see that she did something very like that with us people. There is a scientific name for species that do something new with their juvenile stage: neoteny.

The planulae continued trying out new ways of doing things to improve their lives. Some of them grew up into medusae without settling down. Others, it seems, didn't even bother becoming medusae, but transformed themselves gradually into more complex animals right there on the rocks.

One of the new inventions of medusae was the nervous system. The first nervous systems, made of just a few nerve cells, may have developed from turned-in rowing hairs, which were actually hollow tubes. Nervous systems were a wonderful invention for sending messages from one part of the body to another and really helped get things organized. Once animals discovered them they never gave them up, but just kept making them better.

Nervous systems were delicate, though, and easily broken. The new animals found a way to protect them by running a stiff but bendable tube along the main nerve in their longish bodies. Later in evolution this tube wraps itself around the nerve so it is even better protected inside the tube. When this tube evolves into bone, it gets divided into sections as a backbone that is still flexible as the early tube was.

Long before it evolved into a backbone, the bendable tube was useful in another way. Inventions often lead to other inventions. Long cells that were good at stretching and shrinking attached themselves to the tube and pulled at it in wiggly patterns. That was the beginning of muscles, which give animals a way to move themselves from inside.

Single creatures, of course, do not invent complete backbones or muscles. But we can say that whole species invented such things, one generation after another, each playing their part. The newest developments in evolution biology are showing that creatures change their genomes intentionally through their life experience as Lamarck, a biologist who was ridiculed until now by Darwin's followers, claimed they could. A whole new field of biology called epigenetics, pioneered by people such as Bruce Lipton, is now devoted to working out just how they do it.

We can't be certain whether the new animals, which were becoming more and more fishlike, descended directly from planulae or tried other shapes first. Polyp animals at their different life stages developed into a wide variety of worms and barnacles and countless other designs, so it is hard to sort out a single clear line of development.

In any case, free-swimming creatures with nerves and tubes along the nerves evolved into fish with backbones. Inside their head ends, a clump of nerves had become an early brain. Light-sensitive cells near this brain organized themselves into simple eyes, and mouths gave up tentacles for jaws and teeth.

While all this was happening a step at a time over millions of years, other family lines were busy with very different designs. Many of them kept soft bodies, such as squid or octopus have, with tentacles around their mouths. They, too, evolved eyes and brains. Others tried hard shells around their bodies instead of bones inside. Some shells were all one piece, as snail shells are. Others tried the twin shell pattern of clams. Still others made their shells in sections, becoming everything from tiny water fleas to giant crabs and lobsters. A great many of them discovered eyes and brains and other improvised ways of telling what chemicals, sounds, and movements went on around them.

Earlier we said that animals may be seen as incomplete plants— creatures with cells that have only mitochondria, having lost their chloroplasts. Unable to sit smugly in one place making their food and energy, they must go about chasing after their food. For this single reason they had to evolve skeletons, muscles, nervous systems, eyes, ears, claws, teeth, digestive systems, blood systems to keep it all going and so on and on—all the complexities of animal bodies living mobile, hunting and gathering lifestyles!

Plants, meanwhile, tried out fancier patterns in their own way. Discovering that the sea bottom was rich in building supplies left by dead creatures, some pushed down roots to get at them and grew larger. Others spread out to the shore, where sometimes they were left high and dry. Slowly they ventured out onto the land where bacteria had been living for ages and soil had begun to replace some of the bare rock. Rain and moisture from the soil made it possible to live there and evolve still newer designs, and there was plenty of sunlight. It took a long while to develop stiffer and taller bodies that could evolve into ferns and then trees.

Plants were specialists, as we said, in getting their food right where they were, as polyps do in their own way. The only way they could move was by growing and by scattering their spores, and later their seeds, to the waves or winds, as polyps float their medusae and planulae in the sea. But they never developed the need or the ability to form eyes and brains. Nevertheless, scientists have shown that plants can feel danger, thrill to music, communicate with one another, solve problems and show other signs of intelligence.

It seems that animals took much longer than plants to venture out of the sea. For one thing, before plants had spread onto the land there wouldn't have been enough to eat. For another, they had grown more complex than plants and had to make more changes in their bodies to get about on land and to breathe the air.

By experimenting with ways to meet all these challenges, they finally managed it. Many worked out designs that could go back and forth, in and out of the sea. They were called amphibians, double-lifed creatures, for amphi means double and bia (from the Greek via) means life. Frogs and salamanders are amphibians, though most of the ancient ones died out.

Amphibians are animals with bony skeletons inside their soft bodies. Hard-shelled animals, called arthropods for their jointed feet—arthro meaning joint and pod meaning foot—also came to live on land and later evolved into insects. In the sea they became lobsters, crabs and shrimps.

The first amphibians were fishlike creatures crawling along on fins and learning to develop lungs. Fins had developed from outfolded parts of skin and it took a long time to grow bony legs in their place. It had also taken a long time to develop internal parts besides the nervous system and muscles. Organs for digesting food got more complex, better organized and adapted to new diets. Heart and blood vessels carried oxygen and digested food around the body and collected waste materials. Ears and noses developed for all the sounds and smells the animals had to know about.

Finally some amphibian family lines evolved into reptiles. And some of those evolved into all kinds and sizes of dinosaurs, while a few started out on the road to becoming mammals.

Reptiles, like the birds that evolved from some of them later, lay eggs. But unlike birds, they rarely take care of their young. Their brains are so simple they cannot even recognize their own babies when they hatch. Because of this, they sometimes eat their own babies. They don't mean to be cruel; they just can't tell them from other kinds of food. This challenge to reptile babies made them grow up very fast so they could get away. A baby reptile is almost as good as a grownup one at doing things.

Mammals developed some new specialties which changed the world of animals forever after. But to understand this change, we must look at reptiles a bit more. Reptiles are cold-blooded animals, which means their body temperature is changed only by the temperature around them. When it is cold their bodies cool and slow down. When it is warm they get active. Because of this, it seems that dinosaurs hunted mostly in the daytime, when it was warmest.

Mammals evolved a way to keep their body temperature the same day or night, hot or cold. They also started growing babies inside their warm-blooded bodies instead of laying eggs. Strange animals such as the platypus are early types of mammals that are warm-blooded but haven't yet given up laying eggs.

When mammal babies are born they are much more helpless than reptile babies. They have to be taken care of by their parents or they cannot survive. Their need for care was a great challenge which was met as mammals evolved bigger and better brains— brains that gave the animals feelings that reptiles didn't have, brains that could let the animals learn things reptiles couldn't learn.

Reptiles pretty much do everything the same old way all their lives. Their behavior is planned into them almost as much as the shape of their bodies. They hunt food, show off to win their mates, huff and puff at strangers coming into their homes and fight if the stranger is not frightened away or seems edible. That's about all. They don't even sleep, but just settle down when night cools them.

Mammals feed their babies milk from their mothers' bodies and they are the first animals to sleep and dream. Milk is excellent baby food and also has chemicals in it that makes the babies sleep a lot so they are easier to take care of. Scientists are still not sure just why grownup mammals sleep. It may have been a way to make their bodies, which worked both by day and night, go into hiding by day when the dinosaurs were out prowling around for food. The first mammals were night hunters and slept by day. Maybe dream pictures of dinosaurs kept them just close enough to waking so they could get up and run fast if a real dinosaur poked its head in their home.

The feelings mammals had for their babies were the first hints of what we call 'love' in the animal world. Mothers and babies cried when they got separated, and they got back together by listening for each other's voices. That was the beginning of communicating with voices. The new things mammals could learn with their bigger brains were passed on to their babies. That was the beginning of teaching each other new ways of life, new behavior that was not built into their body plans.

One of the things they learned and taught each other was how to play. Play probably came from teaching babies to hunt. Mothers showed them how to practice on each other without being too rough, and they came to enjoy it. Ever since it evolved, play has been an important part of mammals' social life.

 Mammals, such as later evolved cats and dogs and monkeys, have flexible bodies that make care of babies and play easy. Stiff-legged animals such as deer and horses lead simpler lives with less baby care, mostly grazing on plants as they don't eat other animals, running from predators rather than hunting themselves. Their hooves make them sure-footed runners, but are too specialized to be used for anything else. Their babies run with the adults almost as soon as they are born.

Once again we have been talking about millions of years of change in just a few pages. We have come to a world of rich environments, filled with plants and animals—animals from sea snails to fishes and whales, from buzzing insects to frogs and furry mammals. A world living on the sun's energy, supplies created by bacteria, plants making oxygen and pumping rainwater back up to the sky through their roots and stems and leaves. Countless species of living things depend on each other and balance each other in a great dance of life. The tiniest creatures are needed as much as the biggest, the weakest as much as the strongest, the will to live as much as dying to give new life.

Evolution is not simply a long chain of species, because every link in this chain is part of the evolving dance of whole ecosystems. Each species has its own line of development in the dance of evolution, but all are woven together as they create these ecosystems. Each species, whether microbes, plants, animals or fungi are like organs within a multi-celled creature, each individual like one of that organ's cells.

Although each creature is like a cell within a larger body, it is also itself, with its own organs. And inside its cells are the tinier creatures we got to know earlier as mitochondria and chloroplasts. Even these mitochondria and chloroplasts had their own lines of evolution from ancient bacteria. In this way, every kind of living being is itself, but most of them are made from smaller beings and are also part of larger beings.

However much has happened since Earth's crust began rearranging itself into a living skin of bacteria, bacteria can still be considered the major form of Earthlife. Most multi-celled creatures—plant or animal—start out as a single cell. That is, we are all basically one-celled forms of life that divide again and again in each new generation. And what are these single egg cells or seeds from which we are cloned? Direct descendants of ancient colonies of bacteria!

Think about that! Earth itself can be seen as a super huge cell that evolved two kinds of microscopic single cells: bacteria and protists. All multi-celled creatures that evolved later produce single cell spores, seeds or eggs in order to grow new multi-celled offspring. Clearly single cells are the most important life form we know!

Life goes on and on, for Gaia never stops dancing and inventing new steps. In ape species, the most recent big brain experiment seemed to be working as well as the oxygen breathing experiment did for the archebacs, and as well as the cooperation of bacteria to make nucleated cells, the evolution of multi-celled creatures and the spread of life onto land, outside the protecting sea.

What else could Gaia do with big brains?

She had a great variety of fantastic and beautifully designed creatures, weaving together their different ways of life. And yet, they lived out their lives without ever thinking about them or about their relationships with each other. They knew what they were doing, but they did not wonder where they had come from or where they might be headed. They were rather like actors who had somehow learned their parts in their sleep and played them out with no thoughts of what the play was about.

We will see now that Gaia evolved new steps that did wake up some of her creatures so they could see the play they were part of—could think about it and try to understand it, could think about Gaia herself and understand her ways well enough to help her plan her dance into the future. All this seems to have needed even bigger brains—bigger brains in bodies flexible enough to learn and do many things.

The cleverest and most flexible animals around were the chattering monkeys swinging through the trees, carrying along their babies, teaching them to play, to build nests, to keep safe. We can't be sure just how much they were like today's monkeys, for this was still millions of years ago. Some of them evolved into large ancient apes, the ancestors of gorillas and chimpanzees—and people.

To become human, these ancient apes had to do something like what their much more ancient polyp ancestors did. They had to make their childhood longer and not grow up into apes at all! In other words, they, too, had to practice neoteny—doing something new with their juvenile form.

As their dance evolved, their babies were born earlier, with soft skulls in which the bones had not yet grown together. That way they could get their big heads through the mother's pelvic bones and could keep on growing their brains after they were born.

 Their faces kept a babyish flatness instead of growing long grownup snouts and jaws and bony ridges over their eyes. If you look at pictures of chimpanzee families, you will see that our human faces resemble baby chimps more than adult ones. Are we apes that refused to grow up, like the planulae? Is that why we keep playing and learning most of our lives?

As babies our ancestors needed to be taken care of for a long time. Their teeth came out later and they needed mother milk, warmth, protection and affection. Long childhoods were wonderful for playing and learning new things, and parents had plenty of time to teach them before they grew up and left home.

Home, by this time, was more down on flat land than up in the trees. Their arms were less needed for swinging and could do other things. Their thumbs evolved a better design for doing things with their hands, and their feet and skeletons evolved better designs for walking upright. The big-brained apes becoming human had eyes that could focus easily on what they were doing with their hands, which had gotten very good at holding onto things from all the swinging through trees.

They were, in short, becoming human. Life had come a long, long way from polyps to people.

- 12 -
THE BIG BRAIN EXPERIMENT

The new big-brained creatures began doing more and more human things. They began to live in caves, to warm themselves and frighten off big animals with tamed bits of forest fire. Perhaps they also made friends with them as another way of surviving.

Some indigenous people living today have kept an ability to exchange information with each other and other creatures by what is often called 'telepathy' though a word such as communion might be more appropriate. They know that their ancestors were able to commune like this long before inventing spoken language, just as our cells, and all non-human creatures exchange information with each other. An example of such people are the Mayoruna of the Amazon, as described by National Geographic photographer Loren MacIntyre in the book Amazon Beaming by Petru Popescu.

Tribal peoples who depended on particular kinds of animals for food and clothing treated them as sacred. When we look at the ancient cave paintings of animals we can see the love people had for those huge and powerful creatures. Imagine living in caves as two-leggeds in a forest full of huge four-legged cave bears, rhinos, mastodons, lions and horses during an ice age as early people did in Europe. How could you have survived without having good relations with these creatures? Maybe cave moms asked in this mind-to-mind language, *"Mrs. Cave Bear, will you please sleep in my cave this winter? I promise to keep my kids quiet if you keep them warm."*

Anyway, the first people learned to make fires and tools. They made spears for hunting animals and scrapers for turning their skin into soft warm clothes and levers for moving rocks. They loved and fought and worked and played. They began to invent spoken language, naming things and actions and teaching each other the names. They acted out stories in dances and then began telling them in words. And the more they talked and sang their stories, the more they began sharing things in their minds through this outer spoken language. Eventually most people even forgot the inner ways of talking completely.

By the time people evolved, their environments had evolved into rich grassy plains and thick forests filled with insects, birds, animals, flowers, fruits and grains. A great system of bacteria, funguses, insects and worms were chewing up and rotting dead plants and animals to make new soil. Without their munching and rotting, plants would have no soil to live in. Without plants, animals would have nothing to eat and nowhere to make their homes.

Some larger animals eat smaller ones, and yet there are always more small animals than large ones. Somehow Gaia sees to it that all her species stay in balance with each other as they evolve new steps in her dance.

Every dancer knows that old steps must dissolve so the dancer's body can create new steps. It's impossible to do all the steps at once. A dancer does not mind losing the old steps. They were beautiful in themselves, and they led to the evolution of new steps, but they cannot be held onto if the dance is to go on making new patterns.

Just so Gaia lets every creature have its time, its steps, in her dance. Its plans are passed on to its babies, who create new steps, and then become food for another species or are dissolved at death into rich new soil from which new creatures can live. She manages the dance, on the whole, so that no species kills off another species, even if it is meant to eat some of its members. Just enough to keep things in balance. Nor are species meant to kill off their own kind, and those that do are very rare in nature. Only humans kill each other off in large numbers.

Many species of birds and fish and mammals make their homes in a piece of land or sea they protect as theirs. When other members of their species come into this home space, they warn them with songs or dances. Usually the intruder backs off and leaves. Even if there is a fight, the intruder knows enough to give up well before he is seriously hurt or killed.

Animals use such ritual dances and harmless fights to win and protect their mates, as well as to keep their homes safe for raising babies. Such rituals are like a system of rules for living peacefully together. They help balance things by spreading creatures out in their own homes without crowding, so that all will get enough food.

Living things also make homes for each other, as when birds and insects live in trees, or fish live among the forest-like colonies of coral animals. In every environment we look at, we see species depending on each other in complicated ways, and challenging each other to new, creative ways of living and evolving.

We already know that our own distant ancestors lived in trees, swinging themselves along by their arms and mostly eating fruits and nuts. Probably they were fairly peaceful creatures, as their other descendants, gorillas and chimpanzees, are even today as long as they are allowed enough territory for their needs. As they came down from the trees, into a new environment on the ground, they faced many new challenges and had to figure out new ways to live. In many ways their bodies were weaker than other animals their size, so they had to depend on their even bigger brains to solve their problems.

The other animals in their environment were doing more or less the same things all the time. The patterns of their behavior were largely innate, meaning they were born with the information on how to do things, including how to teach their young what they did not know on their own. Innate behavior patterns make it possible for animals to know what to eat and how to get it, how to spin webs or build nests, how to win mates and care for babies, how to get along with each other.

The bodies and the brains of animals, however, got more complex as they evolved, so of course their behavior got more complex as well. Gradually, larger more complex brains freed animals from some of their innate behavior patterns and let them learn new things by their own experience.

Human brains evolved faster than brains ever had before. We might say that they were Gaia's experiment in giving animals more freedom than they had ever had before. It is as if she is a wonderful mother, working day and night through all the ages, making an endless variety of children, watching to see that they live in harmony with each other, and finally trusting them to learn by experience and live their own lives by their own decisions or choices. It was a very big step in the dance of evolution—a step that was wonderful in some ways and led to problems in other ways, as we will see.

Early humans did not have life easy. Their furry coats got thinner and thinner, their babies got more and more helpless as they were born earlier. But these babies' soft heads made it possible for their brains to grow very much larger after birth. In the first year of a human baby's life its brain grows three times bigger and passes the size of chimpanzee and gorilla brains! And all the time it is growing, the baby is learning new things.

Living on the ground, early humans added fish and the meat of large animals to their diet of insects, worms, small animals, fruits and nuts available in trees. They had no sharp claws or long teeth, so they used their flexible fingers and clever brains to make digging and cutting tools and weapons. The extra food helped them keep warm, and the skins of big animals could be turned into warm clothes. Every weakness they had made them push their brains to work harder and grow bigger.

One of the important ways in which they overcame their weaknesses was by living and working together in larger groups. Hunting was easier in teams and a single fire could warm and protect many people. Doing things together pushed their brains even harder—to develop language, new tools and new ways of doing things. In this way, a balancing dance evolved between brains and behavior.

The challenges of body weakness and survival in a variety of environments pushed brains to become bigger and better at learning. The bigger brains, in turn, made new solutions to problems possible. We do not yet know how many different species of early humans evolved—we know of several, though only one survived.

The history of humans is a story of competition and cooperation. Just as in all nature, learning to cooperate maturely has been the most important part of their lives from the very beginning. Families and groups of families shared their caves and their ways of life, travelled together when food got scarce. We can imagine them dancing with joy when food was plentiful, frightened and anxious when larger animals prowled or fires started by lightning near their homes. Sharing joys and dangers brings people closer together.

 The first people who carried burning sticks to their caves, learned to feed the flames more wood without letting them spread, and learned to cover the coals with ashes so they could be relit the next morning. They were surely proud and happy to share their discoveries with others.

Many things were shared including the sounds they made and the meanings they gave them as they developed spoken languages. We will never know how long people learned from each other just by imitation and mind-to-mind communion before they invented language communication. But surely teaching and learning changed when they could talk about things.

Ancient bacteria had gotten together to do different jobs within the same cell walls, and cells had learned to divide up the jobs in a colony to become many-celled creatures. Just so, people learned to organize themselves into communities where different people did different jobs. Some hunted while others scraped skins clean to make clothes. Others learned to make pots from clay and then to bake them hard in fires. Some were especially good at making up dances and telling stories, others cared for children or led the ceremonies in which they thanked Earth for her gifts. The more people learned, the more there was to do, and some people became leaders who organized jobs and made decisions when the others didn't agree about how things should be done or by whom.

In this way, people came to live in organized societies, though they were not the first creatures to do so. Some insects, such as bees, ants and termites live in organized communities doing different jobs. Insects have evolved ways of building cities, making farms to raise plants and other insects for food, telling each other what to do, and even making wars and capturing slaves. They have queens, soldiers and workers, each with their own jobs. Like people, they need each other and cannot live alone. A bee or ant all by itself loses its appetite, gets sick and dies. It's no use trying to keep a single ant as a pet.

Some social insects have been doing these complicated things for millions of years. But they do them entirely by innate patterns of behavior. They cannot do them any other way. A worker ant cannot change its mind and become a soldier; a queen cannot change her mind and run things differently.

With people, it is sometimes very hard to tell which things we still do innately and which we do by choice. Innate programs still seem to make us run from danger and feel love for babies we see for the first time, or seek food and a place to lie down when we are hungry and tired. We don't have to think much about such things. But no innate behavior sends us to school, or tells us to how to do a certain job, or make up a song. Or any of the other thousands of things we do by learning and choice. We are the freest creatures on Earth.

Sometimes all this freedom makes life difficult. Innate behavior patterns do not stop us humans when we have enough land and food, so we often want and take more than we need. We have none of the innate rituals other animals have to stop us from killing our own kind or destroying our ecosystems.

If you watch puppies or kittens fight, you see that the loser can signal "I give up" by throwing itself on its back and baring its throat. The attacker does not then bite its throat, but walks away. That is an innate limit to fighting that humans do not have. Our lack of the built-in limits other species have has made us an ever more dangerous species—dangerous to other species, to ourselves and to Gaia.

This makes us a very risky big-brain experiment—maybe as dangerous as the bluegreen bacteria that created the oxygen crisis billions of years ago. Like oxygen, we are destructive. But we also bring to Gaia some wonderful new realities and possibilities. We are the first species that can recognize her, name her, learn about her, think about her and actively show our love for her—the first species that can understand its part in her dance, learn from its mistakes and make plans to do better in the future. We may even be able to help her spread her dance to other planets.

Gaia's experiments in new ways of life don't always survive. One kind of large creature that seemed more successful than any which had come earlier was dinosaurs. Dinosaurs spread far and wide over Earth and were indeed successful for a long, long time compared with how long we have been around. When we think about dinosaurs, they frighten us with their unthinking reptile power. Yet we are fascinated by it and sometimes even jealous of it. We make up stories about people going back to the age of dinosaurs and killing them, to show that we are an even more powerful species than they were.

Giant dinosaurs are now extinct. What happened? Their especially great size and power proved to be their weakness. Maybe that is what we should learn from them as we develop our own power to destroy each other and much of our planet. Relying on power, they lacked flexibility to adapt when massive climate crisis faced them.

Our brains and our bodies began becoming human about three million years ago. If that seems a long time, consider that dinosaurs walked Earth for nearly two hundred million years, and had been gone for sixty million years when people came on the scene. That means dinosaurs walked Earth forty times as long as we humans have.

We might also do well to remember that the crisis dinosaurs faced, and which destroyed them, was not of their own making. Theirs was caused from outside Earth, while we have created our own. It remains to be seen whether we will change fast enough to stop it before it destroys us. We will talk more about that later.

 With our brains and our freedom of choice we can be aware that the record of evolution is inside us and that we are inside evolution, playing our part in the great dance of life. We can talk to each other about these things and plan ways of making our important part in the dance more balanced, creative, sustainable and harmonious. We must show Gaia that the risk she took in letting us evolve our big brains and their freedom was a risk worth taking!

- 13 -

PEOPLE IN THE DANCE

Think of the nearly four billion years it took for Earth and its creatures to evolve. Now imagine that long stretch of time as though it were packed into a single twenty-four hour day. You would then find that humans have only been around for the last minute of the last hour of that day. And only in the last second of that minute would you find people forming settled societies. That makes it clear how new we are in Gaia's Dance.

When we look at ourselves in the world of today, it's hard to think of ourselves as natural animals. But from Gaia's point of view that's just what we are, and very new ones at that. By far the most of human life on Earth was not very different from the lives of other mammals. We, too, were sheltering and caring for our young, gathering fruits and nuts, hunting in packs for food, protecting our homes and relaxing in them to play with each other before we fell asleep to dream our dreams.

About a dozen times since we humans evolved, Gaia's temperature fell and great patches of ice spread from the poles into parts of Earth that were usually warmer. We call them the great ice ages. Each time the ice melted again, rich new forests and grasslands grew in its place. Scientists now know that ice ages and the warmer times between them are a regular cycle, or have been, at least, in the past few million years. Ice ages occur about every one-hundred thousand years, and we have been due for one soon.

Hot ages have also happened to Earth, but only a few times, and never since we humans evolved—until now, that is! Suddenly, it seems we are about to experience a hot age instead of the expected ice age! Scientist began warning us of this possibility back in the 1970s, but very few people paid attention. Most people had never even heard of a hot age.

During ice ages, the seas are much lower because the ice gets made from water. Land that is usually under water along tropical coasts then dries out as the seas recede, balancing the land that gets covered in ice closer to the poles. Temperatures in the tropics become very comfortable for humans during ice ages; new forests grow on the fertile land that was beneath the seas. Then, when the ice retreats, fertile land is exposed where the glaciers had covered it and had ground rich minerals into it from rocks they pushed along while they were growing.

Ice ages are only a few degrees of temperature colder on average than the temperatures between ice ages. In a hot age, the temperature rises only a few degrees and everything goes in the opposite direction along with the temperature. The polar ice melts away, leaving fertile land where it recedes and the seas rise higher from evaporated and melted ice. Thus Gaia's natural rhythms insure that land renews its fruitfulness again and again in various parts of her body. The trouble now is that we humans are bringing on the first hot age to happen since we evolved, and we will talk more about that later.

During the last ice age, people were doing well in the tropics and wandered farther and farther to find more homes. Some even lived in caves in very cold and snowy forests in places such as southern Europe where they left those beautiful paintings of animals we talked about earlier on cave walls, showing us that they lived among mammoths, giant cave bears, horses, rhinos, wolves, large deer and other big mammals.

At the end of the last ice age, people wandered even farther into the new fertile places exposed by retreating ice. After the dozen or so ice ages people have survived, we had spread ourselves out over much of Earth.

In places where the weather was good and food plentiful, people organized themselves into settled villages and towns. They learned to make metals from minerals in the ground for decorations, utensils and stronger tools and weapons. They learned to plant seeds and raise their own food, and to keep herds of animals for milk and meat and wool. From the wool they learned to spin yarn and weave cloth. They made houses of wood and stones and then clay bricks, and furniture of wood. They danced and sang and made musical instruments to celebrate their good fortune. They began to speak and tell stories about nature and about themselves. Some were true and some were invented to exaggerate and boast, or to explain things that were hard to understand.

 Nature was good to them, but it also had the power to destroy and take lives, so they both loved and respected it. Like people, Gaia seemed to have her sunny and stormy moods, along with her cycles of life and death. It never occurred to people that nature was not alive.

Most early human societies saw nature as a great mother, and different ones gave her different names. Once language was written, we could discover that they had called her Inanna, Ishtar, Astarte, Isis, Matrona, Coatlique and many other names. In ancient Greece they called her Gaia, and also Eurynome and Pandora, which means 'giver of all gifts'. People thanked the great mother goddess and prayed to her for favors. Seeing and feeling her creative dance in so many ways, they also gave the names of lesser gods and goddesses to winds and seas, to the sun and moon, to the animals most important to people.

They must have felt good about figuring things out, helping each other in cooperative ways and teaching their children how to live better and better over many generations. But they can't have felt good all the time. They also got frightened or sad, sick or scrappy. In some ways that was good, too, for it made them more inventive. They built stronger houses, made ever more kinds of tools, clothing and pottery, created paintings and sculptures, buried their dead with gifts for an afterlife. They found ways to make medicines from plants and learned to grow more and more foods. They learned to make canals to bring water from rivers to fields and built boats to carry things up and down rivers or coasts for trading with other humans.

The first settled societies we know about so far, in the Middle East, as well as in northern Europe, and the Amazon, seem to have been peaceful. They show neither walls nor weapons. Sooner or later, however, such peaceful societies, at least in Eurasia, were invaded by more aggressive wandering tribes who came from colder climates in search of better places to live. These tribes often moved about with herded animals seeking new land to graze. They worshiped father gods, because they feared the power of storms and saw powerful sky gods hurling thunder and lightning.

When these powerful tribes invaded the settled societies and stayed to rule them, they sometimes made the mother goddess of that society the wife or daughter of their sky god, whom they saw as more powerful. Some of them made up new stories in which the god was great and the goddess only an evil woman making trouble. That's what happened to Pandora. Her name still means 'giver of all gifts,' but in the story we usually hear she only brings troubles into the world by disobeying the father god. Some say the story of Eve, the serpent and the apple was another version of that same story.

Earlier, we saw a pattern of maturation in evolution, when competitive species from ancient bacteria to protists and multi-celled creatures discovered the advantages of cooperation and matured by building larger social units or cooperatives that became new creatures and whole new ecosystems. Just so, early humans formed cooperative tribes, and later alliances between different tribes. When this happened they built the first urban centers, for cooperative trade, or cooperative worship of deities, or both.

In such cooperative societies, divisions of labor were organized, just as in the nucleated cells. Only now are we discovering them, for example in the Amazon, in the Orkney Islands of northern Scotland and in the Middle East. Some probably came about when a cooperative relationship was seen between a god and goddess.

Now here is where the parallels with biological evolution become really fascinating! The new cooperative urban centers—just like the nucleated protist cells, and later the first multi-celled creatures—

were new living entities on Earth, and so they, too, had to go through their own youthful phase of creative, competitive expansion! Humans, in short, were entering the Age of Empire. Some of the new urban societies in which settled mother goddess worshippers and more warlike father god worshippers had learned to cooperate with each other now formed armies. Growing strong that way, they attacked and fought other urban centers, or 'city states.' Afterwards, the losers became part of the winners' empires and had to obey their emperors. That way, ever larger empires were formed in China and Persia, Egypt and Greece, Africa, Mexico and South America.

In large empires, it was not easy to keep people organized and cooperating. Emperors or kings and queens developed strict laws for people to obey and used their armies as police to keep order within their empires. Rulers often claimed they were chosen by the gods, or even that they were gods themselves, to make the people believe in their power and obey them. Some of the people in these more complex societies were trained to be priests of the new religions, others turned into workers or slaves who mined gold and silver and precious stones from Earth, or built great palaces and temples for their rulers and gods. Others became metal workers, potters or peasant farmers who grew food in wide belts around the cities.

More riches were taken from conquered peoples. As empires grew larger and richer in this competitive empire-building lifestyle, people slowly forgot about worshipping nature. They no longer knew themselves as natural beings and were told that they were created by their God and meant to be obedient to that God and the human rulers he had chosen to rule over everything on Earth. After all, they could tame its animals, mine its metals, grow their own food in its ground, sail its seas, and grow ever more powerful by using nature in such ways. They grew more interested in conquering nature, forgetting they were only a small part of it themselves.

Eventually, empires grew into nations, and continued the empire age with national empires, such as the Dutch, British, French and other European nations that began colonizing far and wide, even on continents far from them, such as Africa and America. Human society was (and is) still in the competitive expansion phase. Today we are in the third phase of empire with corporate empires larger than most nations! But let us not get ahead of our story...

The only people who kept on believing that nature was alive and sacred, that plants and animals were their relatives and that the great Earth Mother must be respected, were the native people who kept on living in small societies, depending on their natural environments and doing little to change them. Very few of these survived in the age of empire building.

One that did survive into the colonial empire era was the Haudenosaunee League of North America. European settlers found this complex cooperative society of six, later seven, indigenous nations living in lands they claimed to discover and called its people the Iroquois Indians. Benjamin Franklin, a founding father of the United States of America, had the greatest respect for their complex but peaceful political organization. He talked his fellow founders into modeling the US Constitution on the Haudenosaunee Great Law of Peace.

The only problem was that the colonists left out some of the most important things in that cooperative society's laws: the equal role of women, the concern for future generations and the need to give back to nature for everything taken from it. They also decided that voting was better than having to make decisions by working out peaceful cooperation through long dialogues as the Indians did.

Back in Europe, and back once more in time, some early philosophers had spent a lot of time thinking about the harmonies of nature and how people could learn from them, as did native peoples in other parts of the world. The word 'philosopher' means 'lover of wisdom,' from the Greek words philos, friend or lover, and sophia, wisdom. Many early philosophers believed that people grow wiser only when they understand the balancing dance of nature and fit their own lives into it harmoniously.

Such philosophers, who watched nature closely to see how it works, were also the first scientists. Their intention for science was to gain guidance in human affairs by studying the ways of nature. Sadly, that intention, both noble and practical, got lost with time and empire building.

One of the places where such ancient philosophers gathered to talk to each other was the city of Athens in Greece. Athens had a seaport for trading goods with other lands. Along with the goods coming in on ships, came news of other lands and how people lived there. So, the philosophers heard of great empires, such as Egypt and Persia, where kings and queens made all the laws to keep order among the people. This seemed to them a worse way to live than in Greece, where kings had ruled only small kingdoms separated by mountains and seas, and had mostly been overthrown.

Philosophers wanted order and harmony among people, but the men chosen to rule in place of kings couldn't keep order for long either. One after another, they were overthrown by others who thought they could do better and convinced people to support them, at least for a while. But always new arguments developed about who should rule.

The philosophers kept asking, "How can order and harmony be brought to human life?"

As they watched nature, they saw beautiful order and harmony in the patterns of stars and planets, in the cycles of seasons, in the designs of plants and animals. Everything in nature seemed to play its part without being told what to do—as if everything willingly obeyed invisible laws.

Wherever there was disorder in nature, order quickly reappeared. Birds and worms ate up dead animals, old leaves disappeared into new rich soil, rain made droopy plants grow healthy and flower, new forests grew from burned ones. Nature always made order out of chaos. The Greek word chaos had meant the great nothingness (no-thing-ness) from which the universe, which they called cosmos, was apparently created. Later it came to mean the disorder from which nature made order.

Human society did not seem to work like the rest of nature. People were always getting into arguments and messes they couldn't straighten out without fighting. But more and more, philosophers and politicians in ancient Greece agreed that strong kings or dictators were not the way to the orderly freedom people longed for.

It was clear that human minds were able to think and to make choices or decisions. That was a beautiful freedom animals did not have. Yet philosophers saw that freedom got people into trouble if they did not use it wisely. Using it wisely, people would have to take the responsibility of fitting their own free choices into the greater harmony and balance of the whole society.

We have already seen that these ideas are very similar to what the Haudenosaunee had worked out in their Great Law of Peace. In ancient Greece it became the concept of a cooperative democracy, in which people made up their own rules of living by agreement with each other. They, too, as we just saw, noticed that nature seemed to have rules of balance and harmony so that changes could keep on happening without things falling apart. "Would people be able to agree on rules of balance and harmony for themselves?" the Greek philosophers asked.

Balance in society would mean all citizens taking equal part and responsibility in how things were run. Harmony would mean a love of the good life not only for yourself but for everyone else, too. That kind of harmony, they felt, depends on ethics, because ethics is what we call the ways people decide what is good or bad for everyone.

Greek philosophers, politicians, poets, artists, musicians and even athletes all began working together to teach people balance, harmony and ethics. The Greeks loved dancing and going to see plays in huge outdoor theaters. These plays were stories—both comic and tragic—that taught the ideas of making order out of chaos in human life by free choice.

Beautiful, harmonious designs were used to build buildings and to decorate them with columns and statues. People made their own bodies more beautiful and balanced by practicing sports and having great contests of skill—the Olympic Games. They organized a democratic government made up of free male citizens, though slaves and women were excluded.

Today, the world still calls that time the Golden Age of Greece, and many of our best modern ideas have come from it. Unfortunately, this golden era was marred by slavery and lack of equality for women, making the Haudenosaunee more advanced in that sense. Nevertheless, the Greeks were trying to make themselves better and more peaceful and loving by their own free choice—something that has proved very difficult throughout the age of empires that is only now ending, as we will see later.

Certainly things had changed greatly since the time when the Great Goddess was worshipped by farming societies based on nurture and run peacefully by women in partnership with men. The last society of that kind seems to have been the Minoan culture of Crete that left us great palace and village ruins, beautiful frescoes of flowers and birds, bull dancers and snake goddesses, before it was destroyed in a huge volcanic eruption.

In the end, the Greeks were conquered by the Roman empire and later by the Ottoman Turkish empire. Nevertheless, the best ideas of the Athenian democracy lasted through all the ages and all the wars from then till now. We are still trying to get people to cooperate with each other more than we compete with each other. Nowadays, most people worldwide agree with the ancient Greeks that people need a cooperative government of citizens, but they still do not find it easy to organize and maintain such governments.

The idea of being perfect is a human idea that was probably born in ancient Greece, among the later philosophers, who were also mathematicians. Socrates' famous philosopher student Plato, who came to believe in a single god, said God was always doing geometry. Plato believed that nature was perfectly geometrical behind the messy 'illusion' our eyes and ears show us.

But these later philosophers were mistaken when they thought that nature was perfect. They could not see that the stars and planets do not move in perfect circles, and they had forgotten what a few earlier philosophers knew—that nature forever changes itself through evolution, forever works to make order out of chaos in its dance. It is indeed an endless dance, and neither nature nor its people will ever reach perfect order. Nor would we like that, for in perfect order there would be no change. Life is always a balancing act, a dance between chaos and cosmos, messiness and perfection—that is what makes it creative, alive, evolutionary!

Modern scientists have learned that nature must forever reorganize and rebalance itself as things get more complex, and as things keep getting unbalanced one way or another. Gaia is a living being, always rebalancing gases in the atmosphere, minerals in seas and soil, species in environments. Her way is not to reach perfection, but to go on and on creating new life and new organization of life as needed. Yet we see repeating patterns such as the maturation cycle in which living things, as individuals, as species, as ecosystems and as human societies must go through a youthful expansion phase before they can mature in a more stable cooperative way.

When history finally brings us up to the European machine age we spoke of at the beginning of this book, people still believed the Greek, later Christian, idea that humans should become perfect. Even if nature could not be perfect, they thought, humans could invent perfection for themselves. A perfect society with a perfect government should run like a well-oiled machine, they reasoned. They had forgotten they were part of nature. Instead, they had come to believe they were special beings put in charge of nature by God, the Grand Engineer of all nature. They also seemed not to notice that even their most perfect machines developed problems and broke down.

Perfection is such an unnatural idea that, much as people think they want it, they have trouble imagining what it would be like. When they try, they call it `heaven'—everyone who gets there being perfect angels, sitting on clouds, smiling at each other, singing and playing golden harps forever. But anywhere with no problems at all ends up sounding rather boring.

What would Gaia have done without problems? If the first bacterial life had been perfect, no other life would have developed. If dinosaurs had been perfect, people would never have evolved. The whole story of Gaia's dance shows us that problems are not just troubles, but opportunities!

Gaia learns from mistakes, learns to change patterns, to make ever more creative progress. So do her people. People, as we are today, evolved as solutions to problems our ancient ancestors had in fitting themselves into their ecosystems. As people fitted themselves into ecosystems, they in turn changed those ecosystems more and more. Sometimes we think we are changing them for the better, to solve our problems, only to find we have created new problems. We have also changed each other a lot, in some ways for better and in others for worse.

In short, we ourselves are the solution to ancient problems, and we ourselves both create and solve new problems. Very likely this will always be so, whether we evolve into new species or stay human.

It would be wise to remember that Gaia's dance will continue with or without people as a part of it—and that species that survive are those who solve more problems than they create.

Now let's look deeper into some of the big problems we have created.

- 14 -
THE DANCE OF EMPIRES

It seems that big-brained humans are the first creatures on Earth that could understand their part in the whole dance of life. Whales and dolphins, gorillas and chimpanzees, have pretty big brains themselves, but it is hard to imagine them figuring out or understanding the things this book is about. Whales communicate over thousands of ocean miles and chimps are good learners, but it seems unlikely that either of them could understand much about what's happening in our human world or where it may be headed.

Human thinking has evolved together with human doing. The more we have done, the more we have had to think about. No other species has changed its environment so much or so quickly. And none has changed itself so much by changing its own world.

The trouble with being able to change our world and ourselves more than other creatures is that it makes us think we are very special and better than all the others. We think we are in charge and forget how much we depend on them. In this sense, ancient humans were wiser than modern ones, even if they did less, as may also be the case with some native peoples surviving today.

In the past few hundred years we may have done more to change ourselves and our world than in the two, or at most three, million years before them that we understand ourselves to have been human. We call this very recent time the age of scientific, technological and information progress. Technology is, of course, the building of machines and systems of machines such as telephone or television networks, the Internet, air or ground or even space transportation systems, and so on.

Up until this new age of technology, human life had not changed very much since the age of great empires got underway. Smaller, simpler tribal societies continued to exist between the empires and even within them all over Earth. Most of the changes which had happened were about who ruled the empires and what lands they included.

The biggest empires, at the time when modern science and the machine age began, belonged to the kings and queens of European countries, such as England and Spain. With ships and weapons they had conquered the people of faraway lands, which became colonies of these empires. Later these empires broke up as the colonies fought for their independence. By that time, the people in them were a mixture of the original natives and European settlers, with some other foreigners as well.

Europe had depended a lot on the rich lands of its colonies, and on the people who worked that land to produce food crops, rubber, metal ores from mines, clothing fibers such as cotton, silk and wool. Such products were sent to Europe, where more and more machines were invented to turn them into useful things. When the American colonies won their independence, they developed their own manufacturing technology.   Soon there were so many machines in Europe and America that fuels such as coal and oil joined the list of important natural materials taken from the ground.

By the time other colonies won their independence, they had become very dependent on selling their raw materials and food crops. Most of their land belonged to people who had gotten rich from shipping them to Europe and America, and did not want to give up their way of life. They sold the food and raw materials as exports, and bought finished products as imports.

Many of the original natives, who had once grown or hunted for everything they needed to live, now had to spend all their time farming a single export crop, or mining a single export metal or fuel. With the little they earned they had to buy their food. In many ways they became much poorer than they had been before the Europeans had come to their lands. They lost their natural food supplies, and little by little they also lost their way of life—their tribal organization, their nature religions, their arts and sometimes even their languages and the knowledge of how to grow their own food and be self-sufficient.

The way of progress, they were told, was to learn the ways of Europeans or Americans. Instead, life often got worse for them as the Europeans and Americans and their own upper classes, paid by Europeans and Americans, got richer. Many African natives had even been carried off by force to be used as slaves in America, where the Native American people preferred death to slavery. It is estimated that eighty million native people in the Americas were killed or died of diseases brought by their European conquerors from the time of Columbus' arrival. Native American children were commonly taken from their homes and put in mission schools where they were punished for speaking their own languages. Hundreds of languages were lost forever.

If we could have watched this whole evolution of human societies on our planet speeded up—the way we imagined watching Gaia's earlier dance of evolution—we would have seen something like this:

In the warmer climates around the middle of Earth between the icy poles, humans evolved from and among other animals. Slowly they spread themselves out as they multiplied, moving farther north and south between the ice ages until they covered much of the livable land, but covered it thinly enough to make little change in their environments. Then, in some of the best climates, groups of them settled to make villages and fields. In this way they changed their local environments to meet their own needs. Villages grew into towns, and towns into cities and then into minor kingdoms. Wandering tribes came and took over these kingdoms, uniting them into empires.

Within and between these empires, wars were fought and goods traded, building networks of land and sea routes within and among them. People and the goods they produced, along with ideas about living and producing more things, flowed along these routes from one society to another. Great cities became the centers of production and of new ideas and inventions. Raw materials flowed to them from farther and farther parts of Earth, while their products were sent farther outward.

It was as though people were slowly becoming a great being, with kingdoms, and later nations, as organs, with shipping routes to carry supplies and products like a blood system, with ideas and information spreading as if through a nervous system.

The making and shipping, the buying and selling, of the human world's food and other products is called economics. When colonies won their independence from old empires, they soon became parts of a new empire system—a worldwide economic empire, a kind of enormous new living being stretching over the entire Earth! It is a corporate empire, because it is ruled by the biggest businesses in the world, the international corporations. These corporations belong mostly to the richest nations and have a great deal of money and power to make decisions about how this global empire is run. It is a being because every country is an organ within it and all depend on each other, for better or for worse.

As the old empire system began to break up, this new and bigger global empire system took its place. We humans, like the rest of nature, were evolving by reorganizing ourselves into something ever larger and more complex. People did not plan to make themselves into this great global being. It evolved as naturally as did our own bodies, without anyone being able to understand just what was happening. Our understanding of ourselves and our history is still rather new.

Even a little more than a hundred years ago we knew nothing about Earth's billions of years of evolution, nothing about the few million years of human development, and very little of the thousands of years in which human civilizations grew. We could not even see what was happening to people all over the world while it was happening as it took time to carry the information from one place to another—until we finally invented faster means of travel and of communication.

Horses and sailing ships gave way to things run by engines—steam ships and trains, cars and airplanes. The faster they went the faster we could go. They made it possible to ship supplies and finished products long distances. They helped us fight bigger wars farther from home. But they also made it possible for people to move around and see other parts of the worlds, to satisfy our curiosities and enjoy ourselves, or to seek new and better lives.

People visited and often stayed in each other's countries, learning each other's languages and ways, learning to work and play together. The populations of countries became mixed. People who had been strangers to each other, or even enemies in wartime, married each other and had children. The old separations of distance, language and cultures were being bridged by ordinary people while giant corporations were taking over the economy.

Quite suddenly, we have speeded into an age where our telescopes show us the farthest parts of our universe and its most ancient history, where our microscopes show us our own DNA and gut bacteria, where we can dig up ever more fossils and ancient tools and buildings and figure out how old they are, where we know what is happening all over the planet hour by hour, even minute by minute.

We can now make and share our experience and history as eBooks and movies and freely shared YouTube videos, where we can look at our whole planet from space and think about what has happened on it over great long periods of time. Even as ordinary individuals, we can text our emotions—as emoticons—to each other instantly and talk to each other by Skype video at no cost. The fantasies of science fiction books have come true—we have created our realities from our dreams and visions!

All these things are waking up our minds and hearts as never before, as we share what we experience and learn with each other no matter how far we are from each other.

While we were building ourselves into a worldwide body of humanity made of interwoven human societies, the things we were most aware of were our inventions and our wars.

We competed with each other for what we thought was control over nature—control over land, other people, and raw materials. We were afraid there was not enough to go around. But competition alone is not the way of nature, as we saw in our story of evolution from the archebacs to our own bodies. The globalization of our world, the speed of our communications and travel, have all brought us closer together as a human family.

At the end of the second World War, we formed the United Nations so that political leaders of different nations could work out differences and make new rules for getting along together. Scientists around the world shared their knowledge with each other, and the arts and music of all countries became known around the world.

There was a great deal of cooperation going on all the time we still saw ourselves in competition with each other. In many ways, we were blind to our own cooperation. If we had known about Gaia, as the cooperative living being of our planet, we might have seen things more clearly and we might have made less trouble for ourselves and her.

Instead, we learned about evolution just when we were most competitive in winning power over each other through wars. Science taught us Darwinian evolution and so we saw our economies that way, like competition between the fittest animals to rule over the less fit. We believed it was natural and right for people with the best machines and the most money or biggest weapons to rule over the others.

The most powerful countries were proud of their 'fitness' and looked down on the very people providing them with food and raw materials, as though they were much less fit. Their part in making rich countries richer, as they themselves grew poorer, seemed a natural part of the struggle for survival. People called it a "dog eat dog" world.

But dogs do not eat dogs. And even the lions we call kings of the jungle do not eat other lions. Their innate behavior patterns do not even let them get too fat by eating up all the rabbits or any other food supply. If you think about it, lions even help protect their food species by eating the weakest ones and challenging the stronger to keep fit enough to escape being caught.

 In the natural world, competition also leads to creative new creature designs, yet none of them would last if creatures did not work out ways to cooperate with and support each other's ways of life.

This is the part of nature we are just beginning to understand, through our study of ecology—or how ecosystems work. In understanding ecology, we are truly beginning to understand ourselves. We are discovering that we are neither special creatures put on Earth to rule over nature, nor creatures of nature fitter than all the others. Instead, we see that we humans are a new experiment—the new big brain design that is still being tested to see whether it will play its part successfully in the ever self-balancing improvisational dance of life.

15

Waking Up To Our Problems

As we wake up to understand ourselves, we discover that all the time we thought we were making such great progress in controlling nature, we were really doing a lot to unbalance the dance. Our factories and transportation systems have poured dangerous chemicals into the air and water. Our concrete cities don't leave enough space for plants to make oxygen and remove smog from the air.

We grow our food plants in soil soaked in chemicals. Bacteria, insects and worms no longer have a chance to renew healthy soil. We try to replace their work with such chemicals that are actually not good for us. We kill insects that eat plants with more chemicals dangerous to life, and find insects evolving to resist them, while the chemicals pollute the soil and wash into the seas. At present we are destroying more soil each year than we are newly planting. That means the world's food-growing soil is shrinking while populations continue to grow rapidly. If this process is not turned around, a great many more people will starve in near future years than do already now.

We cut down great forests for wood and to make new fields. Destroying the oxygen-making plants and all the animals living among them in the forests, we find we have created deserts instead of gardens. Rainforests are great water pumps, soaking up clouds that come inland from the sea and churning out new clouds to send their water further inland.

When we understand this, we can see that making deserts out of rainforests can actually make deserts out of whole continents! Rainforests also pump heat high into the atmosphere, affecting global weather cycles from the tropics to the poles. Other forests are dying because is bringing the poison chemicals in our air down onto them.

The balanced ecologies of our rivers, lakes and seas are ever more disturbed by the polluting chemicals we pour into them as wastes from our cities and factories and ships. Oil tanker accidents pour huge oil spills into the sea, choking off many living creatures from tiny bacteria to air-breathing fish and seabirds trapped in their black goo.

Our reckless ways of fishing and hunting, our destruction of whole ecosystems, have killed off or endangered many species of animals as large as ourselves, as well as those smaller. We are killing off species faster—much faster—than any catastrophe ever suffered by Gaia before!

Only in the past few years have we understood how the pollution of our atmosphere is forming a blanket that is warming Earth so rapidly that we are entering a Hot Age. This is bringing huge weather and climate changes everywhere as the high mountain glaciers and polar ice caps are melting.

As a Hot Age comes on, massive evaporation of ice loads the atmosphere with water that falls in places away from the poles to cause floods, while other areas are too dry, causing major droughts and fires. Eventually, the ice on top of Greenland and the South Pole, which are both huge rocky islands, is thin enough to crack, sliding big pieces into the seas. All of these changes are causing earthquakes and raising sea levels in ever more dramatic jumps.

These changes also cause ever bigger storms and changing storm patterns that bring them to new places not prepared for them. Strangely, while all this has become obvious, politicians and economists don't seem to want to do much to reduce pollution and prepare us to survive the disasters. It seems that the businesses of our Corporate Empire that cause most of the pollution are so addicted to their profits they cannot see that they are as endangered as are all people and other creatures!

Only now do we realize that our industrial way of life has not only endangered and killed off other species, but that we ourselves have become an endangered species. We have been destroying our regional ecosystems and that of the whole planet. We are the first of Gaia's creatures able to destroy what took billions of years to evolve, and that is what we are doing.

The destruction of our natural world by our economic ways of producing things has been something like the messes very creative children make as they invent things. They don't mean to make the mess. They are just too busy and excited by whatever they are inventing to notice how much mess is piling up or how much of a cleanup job they are leaving for their mothers. Imagine a mother finding that her children have even taken apart her vacuum cleaner to use its parts. How can she clean up at all?

This is just what is happening to Gaia. Her inventive human offspring are destroying the creatures she uses to clean up and rebalance ecosystems. There are not enough microbes and plants left in cities to even begin cleaning up the thick smog clouds choking them. All Gaia can do is let her winds blow them elsewhere, where the poisons can settle down or drop with the rain. But here they only help destroy other ecosystems already suffering from poisons in their own soil and water.

We can forgive ourselves for making this ecological mess without realizing what we were doing. But we must recognize it, open our eyes to its dangers and learn to clean up our ways of production so they do not destroy our ecosystems. Our ways of manufacturing things waste 90% of what we take from Earth as we extract useful metals and 'heat, beat and treat' them to make everything from cars to computers, from bridges to iPhones. In only a very few years we throw all these things into landfill dumps, meaning we have wasted everything we took from Earth!

Gaia is not that foolish! All her other creatures make wonderful things at their own body temperatures without any waste or producing any poisons! Spider silk is the strongest, most resilient material on Earth. If we made spider silk cords as thick as ropes, we could make nets to catch speeding jet planes without breaking them. The gorgeous mother of pearl you find inside sea shells is another amazing material made in creature bodies, as is the strongest glue on Earth. A hornet's nest is made of paper manufactured by the hornets and is a building that weighs less than the hundreds of hornets living in it, and does not blow down in a storm even though it is attached to a tree branch by a single cord.

Why on Earth do we technological humans only now begin to copy nature's ways in making things ourselves?

Because we are still a young species that thinks we are smarter than Gaia and so pays little attention to all she can teach us!

Much of our inventiveness has come from the competition of warfare. In every human war, for thousands of years, each side has always tried to invent more powerful weapons than the other. The idea, of course, was to use those weapons to kill as many people as possible on the other side, while losing as few lives as possible on your own side.

Suddenly, in our modern technological age, we have invented weapons so powerful they kill people on both sides whether we like it or not. You might think we would have stopped making such weapons as soon as we discovered them. But people never throw away their inventions.

Everyone in the world is afraid of these nuclear weapons. And yet we go on making them. We have far more than enough of them today to destroy the whole human species—all the people living on Earth, together with most of the other visible living beings creating our environments. The powerful nations that own these weapons of mass destructions get angry with and jealous of each other, putting more and more nuclear weapons loaded onto missiles into still other countries, hoping to win them to their side. Even a small nuclear war between two nations, such as India and Pakistan could so add to our climate problem that a billion people would die of hunger.

Yet government and military leaders still huff and puff like dinosaurs, showing off their strength so their enemies will be afraid to attack. The trouble is that a single person, losing his head in fear, can set off such weapons. What is worse, they can go off by themselves, by accident. If one did go off, the other side would not know it was an accident and would set off their own as it came through the air toward them.

 Frightening as nuclear power is, it also excites people. When scientists discovered it, they felt they had finally won real control over nature. They were making the kind of power that keeps the sun itself, and all the other stars, burning. They were controlling the very thing—nuclear power—that exists inside the greatest stars and tiniest atoms.

They did not think much about the fact that planets are kept at safe distances from their sun stars. Or that planets evolving life work carefully to balance the use of their star's energy with protection from too much of it. The good energy of sunlight and the harmful ultraviolet rays in it are both the result of our sun's nuclear fire. We are at a safe distance from it, and shielded by our atmosphere by what the microbial archebacs learned so long ago.

Our technological age needs lots of energy to keep its machines going, our homes powered, our cars driven, our planes flown. Soon after scientists discovered nuclear weapons, they realized they could also use nuclear power for energy to replace coal, oil and other fuels. Many nuclear power plants were built and still more are being built.

Even when the plants work only to make peaceful power, or energy, their machinery can break down in dangerous accidents, as we have seen happen again and again. When this happens, the dangerous radiation leaks out into the air. This radiation, like the radiation from bomb tests, kills or harms living things. Such accidents have killed many people and affected the health of many others near and far from the accidents. Even small amounts of radiation stay in our bodies and may build up for years before we actually find out we are sick with cancer or other radiation sicknesses. It can also damage our egg and sperm cells so that our children are born deformed or sick.

Such things are still happening to the people of Japan on whom the first atomic bombs were dropped three quarters of a century ago, and now their own nuclear plants melt down. They are also happening to Native American miners who were not protected as they were forced to mine uranium on their lands after warning us not to dig it up! People who have worked in nuclear plants or lived near their accidents or eaten contaminated food far from the accident sites have all been hurt.

There is no safe way for us to make nuclear energy. Even when everything works perfectly, the plant produces waste that is extremely dangerous, the poisonous radiation leaking from it for hundreds of thousands of years. We have no materials from which to make containers for it that will last as long as the plutonium itself. Tons of plutonium are carried along highways in trucks or through the skies in airplanes every year to places where it is buried in the ground. One pound of it is enough to give every person on Earth cancer.

It is hard to see how anyone can say that nuclear energy is safe. People who make bombs and nuclear energy get richer doing it, just like the people who sell toxic agricultural chemicals and genetically modified seeds. All of them spend a lot of time, effort and money to convince us that what they are doing is good for us all.

More than fifteen million people, mostly children, die of starvation every year. Up until around 1995 we were slowly lessening this problem, but since then it has gotten worse because we let profits override wellbeing as a huge gap developed between rich and poor. Half a billion are sick from lack of food, almost half the children of the world go to bed hungry each night, and haven't even safe water to drink.

Yet, the world is producing more than enough food for all its people to be healthy, much of it produced in the poorest countries. Their people cannot buy even the food they grow on land that was once their own and now belongs to others. In rich countries, there is so much food that much of it is thrown away. This is called a crisis of over-production. Some countries pay their farmers not to plant new crops.

None of these terrible problems seem to make much sense. Why don't we just stop poisoning and killing our ecosystems and even our food supplies? Why don't we just stop making weapons that could blow us all up or damage future generations that survive? Why don't we let hungry people eat? Why can't we live in peace and plenty with each other on this beautiful planet?

We might as well ask why children get into fights, hit each other and take things away from each other. The grownups who have created all these problems are still behaving like children or adolescents in the dance of evolution. The empire builders of the past six thousand years have been acting just like the creative, competitive juvenile species we saw all through evolution before each one learned that feeding their enemies was cheaper than killing them and grew up to cooperate with them!

We are just beginning to become aware of what we are doing, and that we have now globalized into a single body of humanity.

16

GROWING UP AS A SPECIES

Young people sometimes see things more clearly than older ones, but find it hard to get grownups to listen. Grownups always point out that they have more experience and that the world is too complicated for simple solutions to its problems.

When small children take things away from each other and fight for power over each other, grownups are quick to explain that sharing makes everyone much happier. And yet, the grownups running the nations of the world and the global corporate empire too often still act like grabby, squabbling children with dangerous weapons and toxic chemical in their hands.

How can this be, if grownups have so much experience?

Let's look again at what experience grownups have. They do know by experience that cooperation is good for children, for families, and even for whole countries. They can even imagine that cooperation would be good for all the countries of the world. Many grownups all over the world want that to happen, and are even trying hard to make it happen.

But grownups also have a lot of experience in competition. For thousands of empire-building years they have been afraid there wasn't enough land and food in the world for everyone. They have believed they must fight each other and take from each other to survive. They convinced themselves that those with the best and most weapons and land were smarter than the others because they had to protect themselves from those 'others'. They even convinced themselves they were outsmarting nature itself.

Competition drove them apart as rivals, but it also brought them closer together. Through the competitive race for new inventions in transportation and communication, they built the beginnings of a new world body of people, as we have seen. For the first time in history, they cannot separate themselves from their rivals, even if they want to. Nor can they separate themselves from the poorer countries they depend on for supplies, but are finding harder and harder to control.

So, the grownups of the world are caught in a situation where they know they must learn to cooperate, but their habits of violent competition get in the way. When it comes to world cooperation, they have no more experience than children. Like children, they try for a while to cooperate and then break into fighting again. Children have parents and teachers to help them learn. But where is the parent or teacher that can help grownups learn in this new experience of becoming a world body? How can they learn that cooperation is cheaper than competition? After all, competition is driving huge profits from the making and selling of weapons and other stuff for fighting wars.

In ancient times, people believed they had a Mother Goddess who was good to them, but who also taught them lessons and had to be obeyed. She was Gaia, or whatever name they called Nature herself. It seems she helped them grow up and form the first cities we learned about earlier. When the empire age began, most people began worshipping a Father God, as we also saw. Much later, in Europe, scientist declared that no such Father existed and that they could know everything themselves! They believed they could control everything on their own, even that they were flying Spaceship Earth! So much for Gaia's Dance!

Let us see how all this came about.

In the past few thousand years humans have built an amazing world unlike anything any species had ever made. When they reached the age of science and technology, men grew very proud of themselves, very convinced they would solve all human problems by being better and smarter than nature herself. They needed neither a great Goddess, nor a great God to tell them what to do. They even began laughing at themselves for having believed there was any being greater than people themselves.

It was a great shock to people to find that the wonderful inventions of science and technology did not solve all their problems. The problems created by violent competition were growing faster than those solved by cooperation. There was war and the threat of bigger wars, nuclear weapons that could destroy all people, terrible hunger in the world and dead or dying environments as we have seen. Now we have added the problems of too many people, pollution bringing on a Hot Age, the fossil fuels causing it running out just when the most energy was needed, and the world's money system collapsing!

How many huge problems can we bear? Can they really all be solved before we kill ourselves?—before we go extinct by our own fault? We are so disappointed that we didn't solve all the problems long ago, and so frightened by the new problems, that we are in grave danger of losing our faith in ourselves!

Let's imagine how Gaia might see us people and our problems if she could think and talk about all this. She might well be proud of us for having done so much in such a short time. Surely she would be proud of our inventiveness, the beautiful music and art we produced, our efforts to govern ourselves and all the wonderful stories we have told in so many ways. Maybe she would be really proud that we had become a globalized species who could all talk to each other on an Internet.

Realizing we don't know everything is a very important sign of growing up!

It is still very new for us to see we are making ourselves into one worldwide body of people. It is even newer for us to begin realizing that this body is inside the larger body, the greater dance, of Gaia. We had forgotten that. What we did remember of it from ancient times seemed to be only our imagination.

Science seemed to us a much better way of understanding our world than ancient myths and fantasies. The big surprise is that we are discovering Gaia's existence in scientific ways. Science itself is telling us that a living Earth is providing for us and now struggles to keep our ecosystems, our seas and our atmosphere balanced, as well as to keep its temperature just right for us.

Ancient people felt Gaia's presence and sensed the movements in her dance. We have seen her with our own eyes! Just as we formed ourselves into one body, we also broke free of our planet and saw it from a distance for the first time. We rushed to look for life on other planets. Finding nothing so far in our own solar system, we began to look back on our own planet with greater respect and love. Now we are studying it very hard, with a new urge to understand what it is all about. And we are finding it is alive—alive as the single great being of Gaia the ancients understood.

We are discovering that Gaia is wiser than we are—that she knows how to make order from chaos. And yet, that she welcomes disorder as an endless new challenge to create new order. She does not seem to want to find the kind of perfection that would leave her with no reason to go on inventing new steps.

Remember that her first offspring, the archebacs, helped her solve the problems of meteors and ultraviolet radiation. They also made great problems for themselves with the poisonous oxygen, and had to learn to solve them by cooperation between oxygen makers and oxygen users.

 Every step in mature cooperation led to more creativity. Remember that the cooperation of archebacs in forming nucleated cells was the greatest step in all evolution, since it led to all the other kingdoms of life after archebacs: protists, fungi, plants and animals. Cooperation led to sexual reproduction, to multi-celled creatures, to balanced ecosystems.

Now we people have reached the point where we can take the next giant leap in evolution—the uniting of cooperative people into one harmonious world body—a body of humanity that can take care of itself, that can understand Gaia and help take care of her. A body that can even help her plan the future!

Think of it: First the original archebacs (prokaryotes) formed nucleated cells (eukaryotes) as cooperatives also called protists, then they formed the cooperatives we call multi-celled creatures we call fungi, plants and animals. Now we human multi-celled animals are forming a cooperative global family—a body of humanity! In every case, we see smaller beings cooperating to form larger, more complex beings.

When we look at life this way over billions of years, then our biggest problems seem to be interesting challenges. We can see why human cooperation—not just in families and communities, but among all nations—is necessary now for our own survival. We can see that the old youthful ways of being creative, greedy and mean to each other worked to get us to where we are but are now out of step with Gaia's dance.

Gaia would go on dancing even if we blew ourselves up or poisoned ourselves with pollution. Even if we destroyed everything but the microbes of Earth, which we do not have the power to destroy, Gaia could continue her dance.

We are the only species lacking built-in behaviors that keep us from overeating, from hoarding while others go hungry and from killing our own kind. Yet we have the freedom to set our own limits by our own experience and free will. We can see that we have the freedom and ability to produce as much food as we like in ways that don't damage Gaia's body. We can see that we are still children, who haven't been wise, but who have wonderful possibilities of growing up.

Each of our bodies stops growing in adolescence and works on sustaining itself at that size for the rest of its life as an adult. No kind of creature can keep expanding past youth, not even the global body of humanity! Not even our economy! It is time to end the Age of Empire and become a sustainable, cooperative global economy.

If bacteria without brains learned to cooperate, surely we can. If cells could organize themselves into healthy bodies, surely we can. All we have to do is look at our own bodies and see how they work.

Imagine countries to be like the organs in our bodies. Friendly countries can work like organ systems—systems of bones, or muscles, or nerves, or organs to digest food. We can see right away that our bodies wouldn't work if such systems made war on each other or took supplies away from each other.

We can also see that it wouldn't do for all the organs or systems to be alike. A body made only of bones is nothing but a skeleton. No system can force the others to be like it. They must all be different, but they must work together. Can you imagine your heart trying to talk your liver into being another heart? Why do we think people of other cultures or nations should be just like us?

Let's think of the whole world's food supply as if it were the blood in our bodies. Blood cells are made in many parts of the body, inside bones. They are carried to the organs above the diaphragm, the "northern industrial" heart and lungs organs, where oxygen is added and the blood purified to make it a useful product. The heart then sends the blood out, to be distributed all over the body as needed.

Imagine the heart announcing a body price for blood and sending it only to organs that can pay that price, while it chucked out the left over "surplus." Some of the very bones that produced raw material blood cells might starve to death. Then how could the body function?

This is exactly what happens to our global food supply. In the body of humanity, the heart and lungs are the northern industrial companies that own or buy the food grown all over the world, process it, and then sell it at prices everyone cannot pay. Rich countries throw away food while poor countries don't get enough. Much food, such as grain, is eaten by rats or rots in huge warehouses because the very people who grew it cannot afford to buy it. What kind of species are we to let this happen?

No global body like the body of humanity has ever evolved on our planet before. It is the only one of its kind, so if it doesn't become a sustainable cooperative, there is no other to take its place. It will not organize itself just like individual bodies—no more than bodies are like individual cells. Every complicated body in evolution has to work out its own organization. Just how we work things out is not so important, for we are free to do it in many ways. What matters is that we do it in some fair and harmonious way that works for everyone.

What is happening with our political ideas and systems? We are so busy fearing and hating each other, we forget how much we have in common. Capitalist and communist countries both built industrial societies on raw materials they got from poorer countries. But one believed that economics are fairer if individuals own competing businesses and the other that people should work for government-owned 'collective' businesses to create a fair society.

Both systems spent a lot of energy trying to convince or force the rest of the world to do things as they do, or at least to line up with them against "the other side." Worse yet, each system fought to preserve itself against evolutionary changes its people tried to make. This was so especially when these changes seemed to be making it more like the other. Capitalists and communists have been afraid of each other's ideas.

It seems that while communism asked individual people to sacrifice their own interests to the larger community, capitalism encouraged people to sacrifice the interests of community to their private interests. Even within our democracies, conservatives, seen as the political 'right', tend to support private enterprise, while radicals, seen as the political 'left', tend to support public programs.

Gaia, as nature, never splits things up that way! She is very conservative with things that work well and very radical with things that do not work and so need changing. Her advice to us is to see a two party system cooperatively, with one side protecting what works and the other changing what doesn't! That makes a lot more sense than their fighting each other.

If capitalists and communists had respected each other's differences, they might have figured out peaceful ways to cooperate. The same is no doubt true of Christians and Muslims today. Yet the people of the world are still forced to spend thousands of times as much money on making war as on making peace! Imagine what we could do if all the money could be spent on making our lives better cooperatively.

A complex living body needs a nervous system to make sure all its other systems work well together. A brain is a kind of information clearinghouse, seeing to it that all the organs and systems get what they need and, in turn, give what the whole body needs. A brain is not a dictator, but a government in service to the wellbeing of every cell and organ. All parts of the body listen to the brain, sensing that it wants only what is best for them, as the brain listens to all parts of the body. A body could not work if the parts paid no attention to the brain or disagreed with it. Can you imagine bones hating muscles, making war with them, or trying to convince other organs to be like bones?

After the two World Wars of the 20th century, people began thinking they were one global body of humanity in need of a brain—a brain to help them organize cooperatively and prevent more wars. That is why they formed the League of Nations that evolved into the United Nations. Like the nucleus in the first protists, and the brains in animals, the UN, at its best, collects and stores information, looks at the needs of the whole world, and tries to make cooperative rules that all countries or nations can agree to. In all the time we have had the UN, we have not had a third world war.

This is a very good start, but we are far from being out of danger. We still don't have enough faith in the UN and are not convinced it is the best solution. Powerful nations, especially, don't want to listen to it and try to undermine its functions. They think it favors the poorer nations—nations they are still exploiting for profits as we have seen. Yet this is exactly what any brain must do. The parts of a body that are sick and don't have enough must come first for the whole body's health. Healthy organs, that have resources to spare, must help them get well enough so they can do their part.

The UN is the world governance organization we have created up to now, to care about all countries, to care about peace, about hunger, about education. Its job is to try to see that children all over the world grow up healthy and learn to share, and love each other. It is our hope for breaking our bad habits of hatred and greed. But it cannot work if some nations quit or say it is of no use, or refuse to support it if world votes go against them. Such things only show which nations are still refusing to grow up!

Once we recognize this and look to Gaia's wisdom again, we will truly begin growing up as a whole species. We will see that the real power of people in this world is not the power to control each other, nor the power to control nature. We will see that these were childish ideas of power, and that grownup power is the power to see and understand the whole dance of life with our wonderful brains, and to make our own dance a harmonious part of it.

We will know the power of seeing much farther than we have ever seen before in our selfishness. We will have the vision and wisdom to understand why we should care for our whole species as we care for ourselves.

- 17 -
LEARNING FROM GAIA

When we understand more deeply who we are and how we fit into the whole dance of evolution and ecology, we will have the grownup strength to admit we have much to learn. We will learn much more from nature, from Gaia, and we will understand our own mistakes in the dance. We will look for ways to make a better life for all people by our own free choices, and we will make them with love and respect for each other. We will love and respect our planet and heal the wounds we have made on it, with Gaia's help.

It is obvious now that our dream of a golden age of technology, without considering its effects on ourselves and our Earth, cannot come true. The kind and amount of energy we use, our waste and pollution, is simply far too much of a strain on Gaia. We forced her off balance and a Hot Age seems to be her way of recovering her balance.

Recognizing what we have done to her, we can do a number of things to restore her health along with our own. We must do everything in our power to stop wasting energy and rethink the way we produce it along with all our other technology. We must look to Earth itself as a clean, green planet that has been powered by solar energy its whole life, throughout all of Gaia's Dance! Taking our lead from her, we can make our technology, our whole technological world, clean, green and fully recyclable like everything else in nature. We can make ourselves harmless in our ecosystems and even good for them!

One of the less obvious ways to do this is to work for greater equality among all humans. Studies have shown that the nations with the least inequality are the ones whose people are happiest. If everyone can meet their needs and no one has outrageous wealth gained by exploiting nature and other people, things just work best.

In today's poorest nations, there are always some really rich people. This is a legacy of colonialism, when foreigners came in and bribed them with money and power to allow the foreigners to take their land and resources. Poor people were then forced to make things in factories for a meager living, or to grow food on huge plantations instead of caring for themselves and their families on their own pieces of land, now taken away from them. Big corporations continue this pattern by mining minerals, cutting forests and industrial agriculture.

.

The global banking system that decides how money works and where it can go convinced the few rich people in poor countries to borrow lots of money. They were told that buying factories, big power dams and industrial machinery would bring them healthy economies. Instead, these things made only them and the foreign owners rich while most of the people got poorer—even desperately poor—as more and more of the land turned to deserts from the mining, deforestation and unhealthy chemical agriculture.

Meanwhile the debts grew larger because these nations could not even pay the interest charged for the bank loans. And you probably know that when you cannot pay off your debts, such as house mortgages and credit card debts, they get bigger and bigger because the interest you owe grows bigger than the loans themselves! A house bought with a bank loan usually ends up costing three times as much as if you paid cash for it.

To understand economics and money better, just Google Annie Leonard's The Story of Stuff and The Story of Money. In a good society that works for all people, money would never be something you can buy and sell to make more money. It would only be used to make buying and selling easy, to make investments in businesses truly serving society and bankers would only be paid salaries for their actual work.

Actually, great religions such as Judaism, Christianity and Islam all forbade money lending at interest because their founders understood how bad it was for people and their societies to let money-lending become a profitable business. But, being in youthful empire-building mode, powerful people just cared more about how it could increase their own wealth and so ignored the religious teachings meant to bring a good life to all people.

As long as such banking has been around there have been recessions and full-blown depressions. In such times, people become creative and invent fairer kinds of money, or currencies, to use among themselves to keep local economies going. They simply print the money, making it look clearly unlike the money banks issue, so that it is not illegal, and give it away fairly for people to use in trading goods and services with each other. During the Great Depression of the 1930s in the USA, there were thousands of such currencies.

To start such a system, the people in your intended economy need to decide on what they have to offer each other and on the value of making bread or babysitting or fixing computers or giving health care or growing tomatoes or repairing furniture or teaching yoga or whatever else is of use to others in your economy. For example, it could be in hours of work on each person's part. Google Ithaca Hours for a very successful model of such a system.

All you need to create your own money is a group of willing people who can offer things each other need and a few volunteers to get it going by recruiting people and printing the money you decide on. In many places a system invented in Canada is used, called LETS, for "local economic trading system." In this system you don't even have to print and give away money. All you need is someone to run a website where people sign up saying what they have to offer the economy. Each person is given an account with a zero balance and every time you sell your balance grows, while every time you buy it shrinks.

In New Zealand, groups of four to twenty families have taken their money out of their bank accounts and pooled it into their own community bank. They lend it to each other, say for a family to build a house, and every time a monthly payment is made to return the loan, half the payment goes to pay off the loan and the other half builds the borrowing family's account so they can continue to save into the "Money Pool" without emptying their own account in it. Even families who never borrow can agree together to make community improvements and feel good about their valuable support of the community, rather than of banks making money from their deposits.

There are many ways we can just begin practicing how we want to live in the future! Probably we will have to reorganize all human society on a smaller scale—smaller, more self-sufficient and ecologically balanced economies linked by the great communications network we now have. Farming organically, with Permaculture or other systems, in ways that don't destroy soil or water supplies will be of greatest importance. Learning from native peoples who have fed themselves without destroying environments will become a good way to learn. The whole idea of profits can be replaced by ideas of caring for each other and Earth, of sharing and recycling.

One very important issue we face is what we want to do with a clean, green economy once we build it. Some people have visions of a future where no one has to work because hi-tech robots will do all the work for us and we can just play and create music and art and poetry or whatever we like. In this vision, human created technology is considered better than nature, so food would be grown in automated greenhouses, fed on nutrients people choose for them, rather than plants just growing in healthy soil.

Are we really smarter than plants to decide for them what they should 'eat'? Can we ever invent a healthier set of chemicals than those Gaia has produced? We are feeding them fertilizers and 'protecting' them with insecticides made from toxic fossil fuels Gaia buried underground to keep too much carbon from piling up in the atmosphere. We are 'engineering' their genes by rearranging them in ways that have still not proven to make them healthier themselves or for us who eat them.

Technology is wonderful in its place, but agricultural technology has become highly destructive in its use of fossil fuel chemicals, nasty feed lots and other plant and animal torture, the misuse of antibiotics and genetic engineering. The United Nations, after studying our world food supply, has warned us that small farms using natural methods are the only sensible way to feed our whole world in the future and that they can do it.

Big agricultural corporations keep such information away from us and lure us into buying their products because they are cheaper. Yet the only reason organic food is more expensive is because the big inorganic food industry is given money by governments to make it cheaper for people and because organic food is local and seasonal while we have been trained to want highly processed foods laced with sweet corn syrup and additives that are not good for us. In today's supermarkets, 80% of processed foods of all sorts have this syrup in them. No wonder we are addicted to it!

Hi-tech agriculture is not only bad for growing plants. Food animals suffer greatly in our hi-tech feed lots, fed unnatural diets, milked by machine, tortured and medicated with chemicals that harm the people who eat them as much as the animals themselves. Hoofed animals such as cows, horses, sheep and goats belong on grasslands that become deserts without them. Grasslands have dry seasons in which the grass dies if it is not richly fertilized by the hoofed animals that eat it as well as having its packed roots aired by their pounding hooves. Many people think cows are bad for producing polluting gases, but they do that only in feedlots with food not good for them.

What kind of experience of nature will people have in a future where they think themselves smarter than nature? It might truly be good if our cars were automatic robots that never bumped into each other on roads and never got lost. And it might be good if the cars and the roads were all made of non-toxic materials and were recycled automatically when they wore out. And who would complain if car-making robots could even replace themselves when they wore out? But maybe we should think twice about our food and trust nature's long experience in producing it.

All this is to say that technology is wonderful—made ecologically and used where it truly benefits us! But it must not be used to replace what nature can do better. Many many people around the world would be happy growing food on healthy natural land and building homes from natural materials that are healthy to live in and can be very artistic in design, because such occupations provide very rewarding lifestyles. There are many new ways of making farm work easier than it used to be, such as Permaculture, grassland restoration, Polyface Farm techniques (more to Google) and other ways people who study and respect healthy ecosystems have learned.

All of us will have to be creative in thinking up ways of living in harmony with each other and all nature—ways of growing up as a species that knows it is cheaper to feed your enemies than to kill them! We can easily learn from the abundant variety Gaia creates within a single harmonious dance. We can understand why Gaia does not seek sameness and perfection and stop seeking it in ourselves. We will have to learn more about how she creates differences and brings them into harmony, lets new things evolve as balance and harmonies work themselves out, instead of creating monocultures one never sees in nature. We will get all kinds of new ideas for organizing ourselves from all the ways she has found over billions of years. And we will find still more.

We will learn to see our organizations not as machines, but as living bodies that care for themselves, yet are always open to new changes. We will see that creative ideas come from differences and dialogues, that competition and conflict can be friendly and healthy, even cooperative without leading to unhappiness and war.

Consider, for example, how the world might change if, in school sports competitions, people cheered the goals made by both teams, recognizing that it takes two teams in friendly competition to drive the excellence leading to making those goals! What if the team making the most points took the other team out to dinner to honor them for having driven them to excellence? Nothing about how the game is played would need to be changed—only the way we perceive the game! And gone would be the tears of 'losers' because no one would lose. Do you know a school that might be willing to try this for a year?

We humans must stop hating each other and aiming weapons at each other. Instead we can help and learn from each other, to share our best experiences and things we really don't need for ourselves. Very likely we will find that we all get richer this way, both in things and in spirit. This is exactly how so many species grew up as they learned that feeding your enemies is cheaper than killing them!

All through history, great religious teachers and philosophers have tried to teach us these things. So have native peoples, but we listened to them even less than to great philosophers of the western world. We have found such ideas beautiful and have wished for such a world. But they always seemed to be human ideas, human ideals, that were just too hard to put into practice. They even seemed somehow to go against our human nature— against what we have been told is human nature because Darwinian competition was taken more seriously than Kropotkinian cooperation.

Yet nature in the larger sense has been putting such 'ideas' of balance and harmony into practice for billions of years. We did not know that the history of evolution is written into our own bodies— into our mitochondria, into our DNA genes, into our cells, into our organ systems and brains, even into the way we are now becoming one big body of humanity. We are just discovering that Gaia's ways are already built into us, ready to be used for our own good, and that we have the freedom and power to find that out for ourselves and grow up as a species.

If we are to become a mature and thriving global humanity, we must give up our violent and destructive ways—to see that they go against our nature, as   all our best philosophies and religions taught.

In Latin, re means back to, or again, and ligio means tying or connecting. Every search for a true religion has been a search for ways to tie ourselves back to our own beginnings—a search that asks "Who are we?" "Where did we come from?" "Will knowing our origins help us become better people?"

We have almost always felt deep inside us that we were children of some greater being, one far wiser than we are. Now, scientists—who often seemed to be denying all religions—are showing us that we were right all along, by showing us that Earth is alive, that there is a creative Gaia's Dance. And they are giving us hope that understanding our origins in her evolution of this dance, tying ourselves back to them, really can help us become better people.

There is a Hopi Indian prophecy that a red and white brother were born of the same mother. The white brother was sent out to learn and invent things while the red brother stayed home and kept the land in sacred trust. One day the white brother would return. When he did, he was to share his knowledge and inventions with the red brother, and listen to the red brother's wisdom in using them for the good of all people and all nature. If he did not, great troubles would be brought to the world.

This prophecy sounds like our history. The white brother—the Europeans and their descendants in other places—has destroyed the native red brother cultures, rather than listening to his wisdom, and surely there is great trouble in the world. A very similar story is told by the Kogi Indians of South America, calling them big brother and little brother. Aluna, the goddess who created the world sent little brother far, far across the sea because he was causing so much trouble. Eventually, however, he came back to cause big brother, the older native cultures, more trouble. He cut forests and changed climate with all his ravages and inventions.

Perhaps, even in our present crises, it is not too late to learn from what is left of these cultures. Many western scientists are now beginning to look at the knowledge and wisdom of native cultures in rain forests, in deserts, on remote islands.   If we could combine the best of industrial world science and technology with the wiser, ecologically sounder, sacred science of native peoples, we would find exciting new ways to move into the future as true brothers and sisters.

- 18 -
THE GREATER DANCE

Our beliefs about the universe and Earth are our choice, whether or not we are scientists. Most scientists believe the universe happened as a series of accidents in a world of pure matter and energy. Some scientists believe God created the universe. Still other scientists believe the universe formed within a limitless field of Cosmic Consciousness.

You can think of a conscious universe as a Creator being Creation, just as we can see that the dancer in motion is being the dance. In such a dance, matter forms within consciousness as a different, slower, movement of its vibrations.

Yes, it is possible for scientists to have very different views on what kind of universe we live in, just as religions have different views of God. One physicist can believe that matter, in the form of brains, produces consciousness while another can believe that consciousness, as Cosmic Consciousness, slows down to create matter, including brains. Exact opposites!

Think about it. Does your brain create consciousness or does consciousness create your brain? You will see the world differently depending on your answer. Many fine human minds have devoted themselves to this question, some coming to one conclusion, some to the other. So, you, too, get to make up your own mind.

Truth is something you always have to seek for yourself. Sometimes gut feelings tell you if something is true. Other times you have to do research—read books, talk to experts, become a scientist or Google for information, or pray to God. But all the information you collect can only give you clues for making up your own mind.

The truest thing there is for you is your own experience of the world. That experience is your reality! And no two people can ever have exactly the same reality. For that matter, no two people will ever read this book and see it the same way, because each person reading it is mixing it into all their own experiences in their own way!

Science gets knowledge by research, by doing experiments to test ideas, while religion gets knowledge by revelation, that is, by information directly revealed in the minds of certain people. Research in science starts with ideas about how things are, called theories, and then tests them in carefully done experiments. But no scientist can make up theories without having some basic beliefs about the kind of universe he or she wants to study by research. If you have no idea what a universe is, how can you study it? You will either have to adopt some ideas your culture has about it or make up your own.

So science always has a set of beliefs as its foundation—beliefs that are not provable. These beliefs, or assumptions, have been different for different sciences, such as the ancient Arabic science that evolved into Islamic science and the Vedic science that is a very old science from India—both much older than the western science founded in Europe. In fact, it may be only by their basic beliefs about the universe that we can tell one science from another, since every science must make and test theories using good research methods.

Let's look at some examples of the kinds of basic beliefs we find in different sciences: Western science holds that we live in a non-living universe; Islamic science assumes a living universe created by God (Allah) and Vedic science is based on a conscious living universe. Western science is based on the belief that consciousness evolves from matter, while Vedic science is based on the belief that matter evolves from consciousness. Exact opposites! Just these few differences suggest that very different kinds of questions will be asked by the scientists of different sciences.

Unfortunately, western science teaches that these other sciences, along with Chinese Taoist science, indigenous sciences and more are not really science. But how can we decide that only one human culture has the correct information about the basic nature of the universe? If we can agree that there is no one true religion, that all religions are paths to God, then might we not come to agreement that there is no one true science, that all sciences are paths to knowledge?

While it has not been possible to prove scientists' cultural concepts as right or wrong, these different beliefs lead scientists to make and test very different theories about nature. We have seen, for example, that Darwin and Kropotkin had different theories of evolution, based on their ideas of the greater importance of competition or cooperation.

We humans have always been story-telling creatures. We evolved mythology, religion and science for telling our most important stories. At the beginning of this book we found an ancient Greek story, or myth, of Gaia's Dance. We noted that it is very like the story of Earth scientists have uncovered in many years of research: that Earth is alive, that it created its own atmosphere and its oceans, that its living beings evolved into us. Myth, that came to ancient people as revelation has merged with science that got the same story through research and was able to fill in far more detail.

Like Gaia, each of us is a dancer and the dance we are dancing. Each of our cells, each of us as a person and all of us together are co-creators in the dance of life. Remember that there is no dance without a dancer and no dancer without a dance. When we talked about energy near the beginning of this book, we saw that every one of us is made of energy, like a keyboard of low, middle and high keys or notes—a keyboard of matter, energy and spirit.

The famous scientist Einstein showed that matter and energy are the same thing, that energy can turn into matter and back into energy. Think of how ice, water and steam are all water in different forms, their molecules vibrating at different speeds, and you can begin to see how matter, energy and spirit can all be forms of the same thing, too.

But what is that 'same thing' or 'something' that can become different things of which we are made?

More and more scientists now agree with much older kinds of science—thousands of years older than modern science—that this 'something' is consciousness, as we just saw.

In this view, each of us is a matter-energy-spirit being that experiences itself—yourself—as conscious through a mind in which everything we experience, dream or think of seems to flow as we dance our lives. Experience is like a river of consciousness that seems to have a past, present and future, but actually, in all of our experience, it is always now. We can think of an experience from the past, but we are 're-membering' it—which means 'putting it back together'— now. We can also think of the future, but only in our minds—now.

Many human cultures have understood this nowness of our experience as eternity. Eternity is not something that lasts forever, but something simply timeless, beyond the whole idea of time—something that simply is and cannot be otherwise. If your dear grandmother's physical body has died, her spirit aspect is still there outside of time, where it always has been, in the timeless now.

The beauty of that is that being pure spirit in eternity she has no use for clocks and is available any time you want to talk with her, and she can appear to you in any way you want to picture her! For you to do that, your physical eyes are as useless to you as clocks are to her. You must use the spirit aspect of yourself—remember that it is part of your keyboard—to connect with her, and thus you must open your inner, or spirit, senses to see and hear her.

You may have heard this is impossible. That would probably be because your culture has been teaching a science of matter that cannot study spirit, because its basic beliefs do not include spirit as part of reality. Western science cannot study anything it cannot measure. You can still try it for yourself if you have not already. And you can practice thinking of yourself as a timeless spirit, too, in case you did not already know you were one.

So, time is something necessary and obvious in the world of matter—time is always measured by the motion in matter—but time is absent in the world of spirit. As matter-energy-spirit beings we can understand both time and timeless eternity. Many indigenous cultures all over the world have understood both without confusing them.

In our world of matter, where time is so useful, we do things that we first think about before we make them happen. Actually, we create our human world this way. If you look around you, everything you see made by humans began as ideas in human minds. And the ideas in our own minds shape our realities day by day. In our dreams we can create whatever we think of instantly—think of a car and it is there; think of a friend and they appear!

In dreams our creation is not limited by time or effort. Maybe All That Is created physical worlds to slow down the process of creation so that we humans could really learn to understand our creativity—to have to think up a car and make all the parts and put them together. In this way we have created an amazing technological world, and we have come to understand our power to create things in the greatest detail. But it is the world of our dreams we must study to see how the power of thought creates immediate effects around us. Matter has the slowest vibrations on our keyboard and material creation is slow, but thoughts are up in the high key vibrations of mind/spirit and so travel faster and have much faster effects.

Have you noticed that on days when you wake up feeling blue because things are going badly in your life, the day is often unpleasant? What about when you are in love and seeing the world as a wonderful place? Indeed it is wonderful when your mind sees it that way, though things that seem magical on such a day may be your own creations. You will always find that your reality reflects your feelings and thoughts. That means 'you' are not separated from your world by your skin, but are deeply held within it, your skin being your sensitive connector to everything around you, along with your eyes and ears and nose and fingers.

Once again, think of consciousness in the high keys slowing down, lowering its vibrations or tones into our familiar electromagnetic energy and then, even lower keys of matter. It—we—are all One! That is why religion teaches us to love each other and science shows us how I am you and you are me and we are All That Is. Scientists call All That Is the quantum field—that pure energy dance they discovered as they looked ever more deeply into our world. That is not so far from seeing it as consciousness.

If everything in nature is like music played on a whole keyboard of matter/energy/spirit, then all nature is within Cosmic Mind as Vedic scientists believe, and so everything is intelligent from the smallest particle to the greatest galaxy and all the beings in between.

Try thinking of yourself as little mind within Big Mind. If you learn to meditate, your little mind expands to know itself within Big Mind. As the boundaries you believe make you separate dissolve, you get your own direct experience of Oneness. It feels so good you will want to do it again and again. You may feel you are held in the arms of the Universe, as indeed you are. And when you open your eyes again, your familiar world may feel friendlier, too.

While evolution biology shows us that we evolved from other living creatures of Earth, beginning with the most ancient bacteria, we can also see that they and we are just as much spirit as matter. Indigenous people saw, and still see, living creatures as their close relatives, their brothers and sisters—as being just as intelligent, if not more so, than humans. Some people believe that God created people as completely different from animals, and other people believe that alien beings came from other planets and somehow combined themselves with Earth creature bodies to create humans. The truth about where we came from is another one of those things science has not been able to answer clearly, so, again, you must choose your story!

Surely, however we began to be human, there has never been a more exciting time to live! We are finally getting to know a great deal about ourselves and each other and to understand our problems. It has made us unhappy to think we were the greatest beings on Earth and still making a mess of things. Now we can see that humans grew out of their first youthful phase in the tribal past, and that we are doing it a second time as we come out of the Age of Empire. There are so many exciting challenges and wonderful opportunities for growing up in every crisis we face!

One of the amazing things about crises, such as floods and earthquakes and power outages, is that everyone seems to know immediately how to cooperate without having to learn it. Clearly Darwinian competition is not the main thing making us tick. But maybe this should not amaze us.

Gaia, in her long linear-time lifetime, has suffered five Great Extinctions. Each of them killed off most of her living creatures when a cosmic catastrophe of one kind or another suddenly changed Earth's climate so much that few species bigger than microbes could survive. Yet, every time this happened, those that survived got creative in evolving new forms and lifestyles, in weaving their dance into cooperative new ecosystems. The living creatures that survived disasters to evolve us have had lots of practice in learning to adapt and live together after these catastrophes. Life is very resilient!

We know that the only creatures in Gaia's dance to create and solve global problems such as hunger and pollution were our earliest ancestors, the archebacs. And they did all that without having the benefit of brains, least of all big brains! You would think that we would use our ability to imagine better futures to solve our problems before they got as big as they are now. But it seems we, too, need the challenge of immense disasters to get creative enough to wake up and act.

We have invented more than enough things to make our lives comfortable, even on a hotter planet. After all, lots of humans learned to live well in very hot deserts, inventing just the right simple technologies to make themselves comfortable. We have everything we need to work together no matter how far apart we live. Never before could we exchange ideas so fast and so far. Yes, we have created the biggest problems people have ever had, but that just means we also have the biggest opportunity to solve them wisely.

We have reached deep down into the atom and far out among the stars. We know quite a bit about our evolution as part of Gaia's Dance. We know that evolution is not a steady march of slow, accidental steps. Rather, it is an awesomely intelligent and creative dance—a living dance with bursts of new patterns and slower movements among its many different dancers.

Sometimes a species reaches a stage where it is out of step and must try out every possible change or go extinct. Other species find their mature balance and dance the same sustainable pattern for hundreds of millions of years no matter what happens around them. Sharks and cockroaches have stayed the same while so many other species, including our own, changed dramatically. We could say they are like bicycles in a jet age—still functioning perfectly well despite all the new creature designs around them.

We humans, as we have seen, are still quite new compared with so many other species, yet we are already forming a still newer and larger global body of humanity. We are taking evolution to a new stage—one in which we are aware of what we are doing, one in which we organize ourselves by ideas instead of by instincts—one in which we can know ourselves as spirit having a human experience, as some people say, and knowing, or waking up to, our Oneness, our presence in All That Is.

We humans are Earth's first opportunity to see itself through a story-telling species' eyes. We have made ourselves a danger to Gaia by believing our own stories that we are smarter than she is. We are forcing her into a drastic climate change to rebalance her dance because it took us so long to wake up to what we were doing to her and to ourselves.

We started forming the body of humanity by globalizing in empire-building mode. Now we are waking up to our destructive behavior and starting to build cleaner, greener economies, putting technologies invented for warfare into use for peaceful cooperation, just as the archebacs did.

Systems designed for global production, transportation and communication can all be used peacefully and sustainably if we reduce their energy consumption, produce the energy cleanly with renewable sources, make things recyclable and otherwise streamline them until they are ecologically sound.

At present, our national and international politics and economics have not matured to do this well, so we need to do a lot of work on those. Powerful nations are still fighting each other for control. They do not yet realize that the cooperative balance and harmony of the whole body is the only thing that can ensure their own health for the future. A global economy must function like our own bodies—our hundred trillion cells each as complex as a city, yet working in harmony.

And let us not forget that for each of our nucleated cells, built originally as cooperatives by the archebacs, we have ten actual bacteria living in our guts and on our skins where the vast majority of them work to keep us healthy! One of the most important things we must do in a better future is to make sure our food supply feeds them well. Otherwise they will not be able to do their jobs of managing our immune systems well for us. Think of your wonderful gut bacteria at every meal and send them love along with good food!

More and more scientific research shows that most of our hi-tech processed foods are truly junk food for them, while a healthy natural diet can cure, or better yet, prevent, most of our worst chronic diseases.

Fortunately, in the midst of our seemingly hopeless confusion of damaged ecosystems, war and hunger, global warming, massive storms, earthquakes and fires, we are waking up to how and why we have created such terrible problems. Fear of not having enough leads to the desire to take more than we need. This has made powerful nations selfish and warlike. Because, as we saw, humans lack the instincts that prevent other species from being this way, so we must use our big free-choice brains to learn not to be this way ourselves.

We have thought we must choose between everyone looking out for themselves, or being so unselfish that we sacrificed our interests for the common good of all people. As we saw in the last chapter, we built two great economic and political systems on these two ideas—capitalism and communism. Both of them exploited nature to build these huge industrial economies, spoke badly of each other, pointed weapons at each other, then said to the rest of the world, "Well, which do you choose?"

Other animals are not asked to make such choices. They have simply evolved in Gaia's dance to take care of themselves in such a way that they are also taking care of their whole species, as well as other species.   Competition among individuals looking out for themselves, as long as it does not get lethal, can lead to creative new patterns. Most species have learned that sharing land and food supplies without killing your own kind is for the good for whole species.

There is no serious conflict between individual and community in other species. Gaia sees that both exist in balance with each other. She also understands the need for both conservative behavior to protect what works well and radically creative behavior to change what does not work well. She is about both/ands rather than either/ors.

We have a lot to learn and fortunately we can learn very fast. Once we see that people's differences are as important as their similarities, and that Earth's resources are plenty for us all if we do not take more than we need, there will be no barriers to our making a better world for ourselves and for the rest of nature. The problems of war, hunger and ecology will almost seem to solve themselves if we give up on our old, destructive ways—in short, if we grow up like so many other species have done.

It is only seeing our differences as bad things that makes it so difficult for us to care about, and share with, each other. We have bad habits of believing that we are somehow better than people whose color, behaviour or ideas are different from our own. We convince ourselves that only our color, behaviour and ideas are the 'right' ones, or the most 'fit' ones. As soon as we think we are more right or more fit than others, we feel we want to attack them—by saying bad things about them or actually fighting them.

Looking at the evolution of Gaia's dance, we saw that people have to organize themselves by ideas instead of by instincts. As soon as we really get this, we see that our evolution would stop if we all had the same ideas. Plant and animal evolution depends on constantly watching the ecosystems in which they live, adjusting their DNA patterns and the work of their proteins accordingly. Every species has its own patterns, but it must fit itself in cooperatively with all the other patterns to keep its ecosystem in balance.

If we look at human ideas as an ecosystem of different idea species with their own variations, we will stop fearing and hating ideas different from our own. We will learn to trust the whole idea ecology to balance itself creatively. Ideas harmful to natural ecosystems will then die out while good new ideas will keep on evolving. There are many wonderful techniques for bringing harmony into the play of ideas, such as at www.co-intelligence.org.

 The living green plants all over this planet use safe solar energy, which never gets less no matter how much of it they use. In turn, these plants become a source of energy for animals that eat them. People can make plenty of energy directly from sunlight, too, as well as grow plants or algae from which to make clean fuels. We can cooperate in sharing the sun and Earth's bounty just as different species in natural environments do. We can make far less pollution and give Gaia time to heal herself of our wounds.

Learning from each other and from Gaia, we can see that we have no problem which we cannot solve. Our problems have come from misunderstanding and disrespecting Gaia. We came to believe evolution was just a bloody struggle for survival, and did not see all its cooperative balance and harmony. We thought each species was only out for itself and that nothing held them all together in cooperation. We did not realize that all species together keep creating and renewing their ecosystems so that all can continue to live.

Out of our misunderstanding came our habits of fear and hatred. These habits have now pushed us to a point where we may commit suicide as a species if we do not give them up. If we do give them up, and exchange them for trust and love, for caring and sharing, our whole future will look brighter right away.

Scientific knowledge made technology possible, but the 'mechanical universe' scientists tried to understand did not touch their hearts. They felt their job was just to explain how it worked, and to leave it to others to decide what to do with that knowledge. They argued that it wasn't up to them to say which knowledge might be good for us and which bad.

As our technological world got into more and more trouble, people began to blame science. It did not bring the golden future people had expected. Instead it seemed heartless and dangerous. Just because it was not guiding us, it seemed to be misguiding us, even leading us to our own destruction.

But science itself is a cooperative, living, evolving dance of human brain-minds—a dance that must try harder to get in step with nature's dance. When scientists thought nature was an immense clockworks, they believed they could reach complete knowledge of how its mechanisms worked. But, as we saw, the harder and closer they looked at the world machine, the more they discovered that it wasn't a machine at all.

The new scientific view of the universe and our Earth as a living dance of energy in which everything is connected and forever changing and evolving —from the tiniest particles of energy to the greatest wheeling galaxies—does touch our hearts. In such a universe, nature never reaches perfect order, and people never reach perfect knowledge. Nothing settles down to work like a perfect machine. We cannot use our knowledge to create a perfect human society; we can only use it to guide us toward balance and harmony.

Our new knowledge shows us that we cannot stand outside nature to study it or to control it. We are forever just one part of its dance, seeing things and feeling our way along from inside it. Everything we do affects the whole; everything is inseparable and interdependent. That is Oneness!

It took us a long time to get from the ancient myth of Gaia to the scientific discovery that she exists as our living Earth and that we are part of her. This discovery is more fascinating and beautiful than any other story we ever made up about our creation and being. We love myths, because they express a deep part of ourselves that is in harmony with the universe. Their poetic beauty makes us laugh and cry with feeling. Myths touch our hearts as well as our minds. As modern science grows out of its machine age, it becomes beautiful in the same way.

We have always told myths to guide our human lives, and we are still making them up—especially myths about leaving our planet in search of other intelligent life out in space. Most of these myths show that we are still thinking in machine-age ways, and in the ways of empire. We want to conquer the universe; we expect others to have super weapons and to make war on us. We think of ways to outsmart them and win these "star wars."

Do we really want to take these empire and machine-age ideas into space with us? Let's think for a minute about what might be happening out there on other planets.

Planets are scattered throughout the universe. Perhaps, like the spores and seeds and eggs of Earth, those in just the right conditions will spring to life and evolve its own smaller living creatures. Each such planet will work out its own dance and perhaps eventually a great living system of many planets together. To do that each of the planets involved will have to fit into this greater dance without destroying it.

Sooner or later, the intelligent creatures on any planet will discover the great explosive force lying inside the atom. If these intelligent beings have already matured to live peacefully together all over their planet, and if they have learned to make their energy in harmless ways, they will leave nuclear power to their stars.

If they are not yet peaceful and wise, they will probably create the same kinds of problems for themselves as we have. Some of them may have blown themselves up, unable to learn love and trust in time to save themselves. Others may have passed such a crisis to become peaceful. They will probably have formed an intelligent, aware, planet-wide system of local governance that keeps its planet healthy—the kind of planet ready to form a cooperative new alliance with other planets in their or other star-sun systems.

Scientists know now that there is 'non-locality' in deep reality, such that things as far apart in space as you like can commune with each other directly, can know what each other are doing without needing the communication of a common language. We have also seen that on non-physical parts of our 'keyboard' time does not exist and that consciousness has no boundaries. Putting these two things together we see that intelligent cultures of beings throughout space have the opportunity to commune—to exchange information directly—within cosmic consciousness without even needing telescopes or spaceships!

If such cultures do come to our planet—and many people say they have been coming to visit us for thousands of years already—then they are far more likely to be friendly than hostile. And let us hope that by the time we find such planets ourselves, we will have traded in our old habits of fear and hatred for new ones of trust and love. Let's hope we will have solved the biggest problems on our own planet, rather than dreaming of leaving it to escape them.

It's difficult to imagine that there are more beautiful planets than our own anywhere in the universe. If other beings from faraway planets come close and see ours, they will know right away it is alive. They will feel joy at its shimmering loveliness and will want to approach us. If they have come in the past, or are coming now, they may sense our fear, anger and confusion. They would know we are not ready to help build a harmonious universal alliance. So they may just leave quietly, the way one would leave a roomful of angry people if one had come to be friendly—or they may just watch us and wait...

The stories you have learned —from parents, teachers, friends, books, TV or wherever—all leave you with choices about which ones to adopt as your own. When you adopt them, they become your beliefs, your own story of How Things Are. Think of your beliefs—all of them, even the ones you call 'facts'—as a garden of beliefs. You plant many beliefs; then you weed some out as you stop believing them over time, and you keep planting new ones as you get new information that seems to work better for you. You plant those that seem to belong together in certain parts of the garden and you try to make the whole garden as harmonious and beautiful as possible, even making room for beliefs that feel like bleeding hearts flowers or weeping willow trees.

The sooner we get in tune with Gaia's dance and make our planet a loving and healthy one, the sooner we will be ready to welcome space visitors—and to go out on our own in love and trust.

We have a lot to do to get through the maturation process in our own evolution, but many people are already hard at work on it. They are working in the peace movement, in ecology and education, in science and health care, in politics and economics, in law and psychology, and in religions and all the arts. Their work is often joyful because they believe so strongly in a better future, but also may seem hard because so many other people don't understand and support them, hanging on to the old habits of fear and hatred instead.

If people all over the world come to love their own lives as part of Gaia's Dance, Gaia's big brain experiment may prove to be well worth the risk. We will all know that we are still young, as a human species and can make the future as bright as we would like it to be. With our love and cooperation, Gaia's Dance will go on in creative balance and harmony—both for itself and as part of the greater harmonies of the whole universe.

THANK YOUs

This book was conceived long ago with my appreciation for the work of James Lovelock and Lynn Margulis on their Gaia Theory of our living Earth and for their personal encouragement of my own interpretation.

More recently I met Betty Sue Flowers, a superb editor/writer who very graciously gave me the best of editorial advice and further encouragement to release this book to the public at long last.

My greatest gratitude goes to Gaia herself as the parent planet that spawned us, however great troublemakers we have proven ourselves to be, and for her great patience with us as we struggle to grow up and become worthy of her.